Spelling
by
Principles

A
Programed
Text

Spelling
by
Principles

Genevieve Love Smith

Research Director of Programed Instruction

Point Park College
Pittsburgh, Pennsylvania

Prentice-Hall, Inc., Englewood Cliffs, New Jersey

PRENTICE-HALL INTERNATIONAL, INC., *London*
PRENTICE-HALL OF AUSTRALIA, PTY. LTD., *Sydney*
PRENTICE-HALL OF CANADA, LTD., *Toronto*
PRENTICE-HALL OF INDIA PRIVATE LIMITED, *New Delhi*
PRENTICE-HALL OF JAPAN, INC., *Tokyo*

To the Student and Teacher

Aim

To enable the college student to improve his spelling in the most efficient manner—with the most gain for the time spent.

Objectives

Upon the completion of this program, the student will respond by:

1. choosing correctly between *ie* and *ei*;
2. doubling a final consonant when it is correct to do so;
3. refraining from doubling a final consonant when appropriate;
4. changing a final *y* to *i* when it should be changed;
5. spelling noun plurals correctly;
6. dropping a final silent *e* when it should be dropped;
7. keeping the final silent *e* when needed;
8. using a device that most good spellers use unconsciously to identify a vowel which has no identifiable sound;
9. correctly doubling or not doubling a letter when presented with a prefix and word-root situation;
10. using *ly* and *ally* in the correct places;
11. automatically selecting which is correct when confronted with an *ian/ion* decision;
12. using *ify* and *efy* correctly;
13. building nouns skillfully from verbs ending in *ify/efy*;
14. distinguishing between prefixes which sound very much alike;
15. applying some very high odds that usually result in correct spelling when a gamble *must* be taken.

Students intended

1. College students who have a spelling handicap.
2. Any post-high school student who is not necessarily a poor speller, but is not confident of his spelling.

Assumptions

1. The student can read carefully.
2. The student can apply (or learn to apply) principles.

Other materials

A dictionary is recommended. Even a paperback that has some bit of etymology following a word entry will do. (*Webster's New World Dictionary* is available in paper binding for fifty cents.)

Validation

All statements in the program were checked against *The Teachers Word Book of 30,000 Words* by Thorndike & Lorge, published by the Bureau of Publications, Teachers College, Columbia University, New York.

Tests

Diagnostic Tests:*

    One form for self-administration
    One form for teacher administration
    (Keys for both forms are included in the Teacher's Manual.)

Pre- and post-chapter tests

Teacher's Manual

Available to faculty only

Time

Average time for high achievement—20 hours (based on students' reported time)

    Spelling by Principles: A Programed Text is an autoinstructional course which is designed to teach remedial spelling efficiently. It is intended for use by college students who, quite naturally, expect to get the most value for the time spent. Not only does this program improve the student's present spelling, but it also furnishes a basis for improved spelling throughout life because it provides for vocabulary growth. The means used to achieve this end were suggested to the author by research done at Oregon State University by Dr. Ned Marksheffel.

    This text presents a *system* to improve spelling. The author does not intend to imply that there is always only one correct way to spell a word. (For example, there are three correct spellings for *arhythmia, arrhythmia, arrythmia*.) This system *does* assure the student that he will *not* misspell a word when he applies what he has learned. The student can also be confident that he is using the preferred, time-honored spelling of a word—the spelling that he is most likely to see in the best writing.

Other applications of the program

    In addition to the intended use of the program, there have been two very interesting applications that developed as a surprise spin-off. One academic

---

* In the diagnostic test, if only one error occurs for a reference to a given chapter, this can be interpreted leniently. There are several items for each chapter. All items are discriminating, but only 72% of the items are highly discriminating. The tests were constructed in this manner to add flexibility to the program. Because of "scatter," a teacher could use one diagnostic test as a pre-program test and the other as a post-program test to measure student progress. This use of the diagnostic tests should be considered only for students who work the entire program.

counselor was working at another institution with adults who had dropped out of school at various stages of their academic development. They differed greatly, but all were highly motivated for learning. This teacher used the spelling program, not only to teach these students how to spell, but also to show them how to apply principles. She is a dynamic, dedicated and most imaginative teacher. The author is certain that there are many such teachers throughout our country who are looking for similar answers. The author feels certain also that there are many students who could profit from this approach.

The other suggested spin-off for the program—helping foreign students to learn English—has had no large-scale investigation. Three foreign students in a class of 25 students taking remedial English showed the following test results:

Results from Nine Post-chapter Tests

Student from:	1	2	3	4	5	6	7	8	9
Afghanistan	38%	30%	84%	61%	80%	85%	90%	80%	90%
Nepal	60%	60%	56%	67%	80%	73%	100%	88%	100%
Nepal	62%	60%	68%	78%	86%	70%	100%	88%	100%

It is possible that a student looking for solutions to a similar problem might want to try this program as an aid.

Testing and revision

This program as it now exists was developed at Point Park Junior College and tested rigorously. The first attempt was tested on three students and revised. This revision was tested in two classes and revised. The existing copy represents the sixth revision, with feedback from the work of very many students who used it either autoinstructionally or in classes under eight different teachers. At one time five teachers were using this programed text with ten different classes in remedial English.

Students who have used this text could be classified under the following categories:

1. *Workshop students*—students who cannot be admitted to the college without considerable upgrading of skills.
2. *Students in E01*—students admitted to the college, but required to take a non-credit course in remedial English.
3. *Regular college freshmen*—students in both the first and second trimester.
4. *A.I.D. students*—students who were admitted to the college as regular students, but who performed below the required Quality Point Average. These students were given the choice of dismissal or of taking a course in Academic Improvement and Development. (If they passed, they were reinstated on probation.)
5. *Adults* in Duff's Business Institute's Adult Education Improvement Course.
6. *Regular students* attending Duff's Business Institute.

The first four of the above categories were composed of students from Point Park Junior College. The last two categories represent students from Duff's Business Institute, a privately owned business school over 100 years old. Texts from the above students were collected and returned to the author. These, plus teacher's comments, provided the basis of the six revisions.

At Point Park Junior College we have had experience in using this text both autoinstructionally and in classes that met once a week with a teacher. When the program is used in a class that meets with a teacher, we have found the best method for producing high achievement is as follows:

1. At the first class session, a standardized spelling test with college norms is given. We have used Educational Testing Service's spelling test, Forms O.M. and P.M. Our Data Processing Center scores the test, gives us individual students' scores as well as the mean class score, and calculates the standard deviation for each group tested. The raw scores are converted to the national norms for entering college freshmen. This figure is a percentile ranking. The standard deviation gives a clue to the homogeneity or heterogeneity of the class in spelling ability. Also during this session, a ten-word pretest for Chapter 1 is dictated to the student, and the introduction plus Chapter 1 are assigned for the next week. Naturally, the teacher has already worked this chapter. If there are students who have never used a programed text, the procedure involved is introduced to them.

2. At the second class session the students are asked if they have any questions before their chapter posttest. If there are questions they are answered. Questioning usually occurs with workshop students only. The Chapter 1 posttest (ten words) is dictated. The pretest for Chapter 2 is dictated. Chapter 2 is assigned for the next class session. The students are given their graded Chapter 1 pretests.

3. This procedure is followed throughout the course.

4. Variables in the above usage are determined by the size of the class and the ability of the student. With small classes one-half period or less is necessary. With able students there are rarely questions. With very large classes the time for administering the quizzes and the time for questions vary in relation to the size of the class and the ability of the student. It has never been necessary to use a full class hour, even with a class of 54 workshop students.

5. It is most important that the teacher has worked a chapter ahead of the student and that there is never an implication of any kind that a student would think of coming to class unprepared.

6. It is quickly evident that, as the student sees his improvement from chapter pretest to posttest, the ten-word quizzes become highly motivational.

7. At the end of the course the alternate form of Educational Testing Service's spelling test is given, national percentile norms are calculated, and spelling progress is measured.

The author is not certain which of the following two students made the greatest gain, but they both represent extremes of progress. One student, a workshop student, spelled in the seventy-fourth percentile for entering college freshmen before the spelling program and in the ninety-fourth percentile after.*

* Based on norms from Educational Testing Service's Spelling Test (Forms O.M. and P.M.).

Although he was not a poor speller to begin with, he said he liked the course because it gave him "confidence." The other student moved from the first percentile to the fiftieth. These students were from the workshop and A.I.D. groups.

The outlined procedure approaches the ideal when a busy teacher seeks to exercise some measure of control of the instructional process. This procedure has grown out of many other attempts to achieve optimum results from this program. The author believes that other equally good methods of application could be devised. Further refinements of the described approach are under consideration at Point Park Junior College. They will probably involve the establishment of a cut-off point on the Educational Testing Service pretest and greater use of the diagnostic tests.

The author not only developed the program, but also worked it herself when she was teaching a group that was using the program in a formal class session. The actual working through the text was a remarkable experience for her because she learned something of what the student was experiencing. In addition, she discovered two fairly important things. Chapter 9 is quite long and could well be done at two different sittings. Frame 64, Chapter 10, page 139, requires a great deal of work, but results in tacking down securely what the student has learned. It also offers, to the teacher who cares to do so, an excellent opportunity to introduce students to an unabridged dictionary or the Oxford Dictionary.

Spelling by Principles: A Programed Text has different autoinstructional uses. Again, efficacy varies with the motivation of the student.

1. Students are simply given the program.
2. Students are given the program and required to report for chapter pre- and posttests.
3. Highly motivated students administer their own diagnostic test, find their own area of weakness, and work on it.

Unfortunately, we have not yet administered the nationally standardized pre- and post-program tests and then turned the student loose. With entering freshmen this may or may not be advisable. The author believes that there is no reason why this cannot be done if the student knows he has a given level of spelling proficiency to attain. So far, however, our teachers have exercised some type of control.

Student response

There seems to be only one more thing that would be of value and interest to students and teachers: *How do students like the program?* A questionnaire was prepared and given to students in a manner that would assure them complete anonymity. It was administered to one group of 54 students. The results are shown here. The "comments" included represent the gamut of responses proportionally as they occurred.

Tabulation of Questionnaire

Did you like learning spelling from the programed text?   Yes   50

No   4

*Would you like learning other course material (content)
from a programed text?*   Yes   38

No   11

It depends   5

*If you care to make a brief comment about this course and/or the
spelling program, please do so here.*

"Although I am taking another programed course, I rate this spelling course first."

"I thought the course was exceptionally good."

"I didn't think I could improve in spelling because I was pretty good, but I have."

"The text, though boring at times, contained much valuable information. In retrospect it was a good course."

"I'm sure I have learned a lot."

". . . very worthwhile."

"I thought this course was terrific because I have learned very much from it."

"I am a very poor speller and your program has raised my standards."

"I learned a lot from it and it has helped me in my other subjects."

"I never knew I spelled so many words wrong until I began using the program."

"It was fun as well as educational."

". . . reminded me of high school, not college. Other than that, it was very good."

"I liked learning from the programed book because it helped me to understand more than if I just tried to memorize words."

". . . at times tends to be boring."

"I believe pronunciation and enunciation should have been stressed a little more."

"It is the best that could be taken in spelling."

"You must learn! However, I cannot; and this is my third time around for programed learning."

"Spelling can be learned in an easier manner, and rules in a way are unnecessary."

"Every minute went like seconds."

The author offers this autoinstructional text with sincere humility, but also with the knowledge that it can and will help a student master an essential skill. Any comments or suggestions from teachers or students who have used this text are invited and will be most appreciated.

Genevieve Love Smith
Point Park College

Acknowledgments

The author wishes to express gratitude to the administration of Point Park College for complete backing in this project.

Special thanks to:

Dr. Dorothy C. Finkelhor, President of the college, for envisioning the need to upgrade students' skills and for electing to handle spelling deficiency by the programed approach.

Dr. L. Herbert Finkelhor, Chairman of the Board of the college, for his sustained interest in the development of and results of the use of the program.

Dean Phyllis E. Davis for providing trial students and for giving encouraging words and a helping hand at the right times.

Mr. Arthur M. Blum, Executive Vice-president of the college, for aid in the mechanics involved with program development and in selection of testing instruments.

Dr. Helen-Jean Moore, Director of Libraries, for her interest throughout the development of the program and her particular concern for its eventual use.

Mrs. Hebe D. Bonn, Librarian, for her personal interest in providing an unending stream of books, lists, articles from journals and anything at all related to spelling.

Mrs. Lois Golden for feedback from her imaginative and successful use of the program in ways not originally dreamed by the author.

Mrs. Carol Frank Wenzel, Miss Karen Wiggins, and Miss Sallie Kearns for secretarial help and critical insight beyond that which could normally be expected.

Mr. Allen H. Krause, Miss Amelia A. Poklar, and faculty, staff, and students too numerous to mention, for suggestions, criticisms, encouragement and all of those normal human daily interests that make the life of study and exploration of new media not only bearable but thrilling and vibrantly alive.

Point Park College for being the kind of stimulating, vital school that it is; the sort of a place that makes one's work his greatest fulfillment and pleasure.

Contents

Diagnostic Spelling Test

Note to the Student

This test will help you to determine any special spelling problems you may have. The
answer key at the end of the test will refer
you to a chapter of the program which will
help you correct your special problems. The
test will not help you with *all* your spelling
problems, however. After you complete the
test, you should work through the entire
program carefully.

Directions: Check the correct answer. (Answer section follows.)

1. *meaning:* "grouped"
   - *a.* asorted
   - *b.* assorted
   - *c.* asortted
   - *d.* none of the above

2. *meaning:* "entertaining"
   - *a.* amuseing
   - *b.* amusing
   - *c.* amusment
   - *d.* none of the above

3. *ible* or *able?*
   - *a.* abominable
   - *b.* reducable
   - *c.* admirible
   - *d.* none of the above

4. *meaning:* "obedient"
   - *a.* dutyous
   - *b.* dutious
   - *c.* duteous
   - *d.* none of the above

5. *meaning:* "to attain a goal"
   - *a.* succeed
   - *b.* suceed
   - *c.* succede
   - *d.* none of the above

6. *meaning:* "a heavenly being"
   - *a.* angle
   - *b.* angell
   - *c.* angal
   - *d.* none of the above

7. *meaning:* plural of an animal
   that is fun to watch
   at the zoo
   - *a.* monkies
   - *b.* monkeyes
   - *c.* monkeies
   - *d.* none of the above

8. *meaning:* "agitated"
   - *a.* nervus
   - *b.* nerveus
   - *c.* nervous
   - *d.* none of the above

9. *meaning:* "the boss"
   - *a.* cheef
   - *b.* cheif
   - *c.* chief
   - *d.* none of the above

10. *meaning:* "a formal parade"
    - *a.* processian
    - *b.* precesion
    - *c.* precession
    - *d.* none of the above

11. *meaning:* a synonym for very
    disagreeable (adverb)
    a. horribley
    b. horribly
    c. horribely
    d. none of the above

12. *meaning:* "ambition"
    a. aspireing
    b. aspireation
    c. aspiration
    d. none of the above

13. *meaning:* "process of becoming
    liquid"
    a. liquefaction
    b. liquifaction
    c. liquification
    d. none of the above

14. *meaning:* "an establishment for
    monks"
    a. monestary
    b. monastery
    c. monastary
    d. none of the above

15. *meaning:* "pessimistic"
    a. cynicle
    b. cynicel
    c. cynical
    d. none of the above

16. *meaning:* "what you learn when
    you step on the
    scales"
    a. waight
    b. wieght
    c. weight
    d. none of the above

17. *meaning:* "one who amuses"
    a. comedian
    b. comedean
    c. comedion
    d. none of the above

18. *for* or *fore?*
    a. forsee
    b. foresake
    c. forhead
    d. none of the above

19. *meaning:* plural for the musical
    instrument
    a. pianos's
    b. pianos
    c. pianoes
    d. none of the above

20. *meaning:* "state of excessive
    drinking"
    a. alcohalism
    b. alcohelism
    c. alcoholism
    d. none of the above

21. *meaning:* "to adapt"
    a. accomodate
    b. accommodate
    c. acommodate
    d. none of the above

22. *Check the correct answer.*
    a. disect
    b. disipate
    c. disolve
    d. none of the above

23. *Check the correct answer.*
    a. antipathy
    b. antepathy
    c. antaseptic
    d. none of the above

24. *ance* or *ence?*
    a. extravagence
    b. intelligance
    c. significence
    d. none of the above

25. *meaning:* "assign"
    a. allottment
    b. allotting
    c. alloted
    d. none of the above

26. *Check the correct answer.*
    a. financier
    b. concieted
    c. decietful
    d. none of the above

27. *Check the correct answer.*
    a. greivance
    b. leisure
    c. preistly
    d. none of the above

28. *Check the correct answer.*
    a. dignify
    b. rarify
    c. putrify
    d. none of the above

29. *meaning:* "grant or yield"
    a. conceed
    b. concede
    c. consede
    d. none of the above

30. *meaning:* increased quality
    a. improvement
    b. improveing
    c. improveable
    d. none of the above

31. *meaning:* "special right or privilege"
    a. perrogative
    b. prerogative
    c. prorogative
    d. none of the above

32. *meaning:* "not private" (adverb)
    a. publicly
    b. publically
    c. publicily
    d. none of the above

33. *Check the correct answer.*
    a. nineth
    b. wholly
    c. truely
    d. none of the above

34. plural of proper names
    a. Ruthes
    b. Gladys's
    c. Freds
    d. none of the above

35. *meaning:* "having qualities of beauty"
    a. beautyous
    b. beautious
    c. beauteous
    d. none of the above

36. words formed from *transfer*
    a. transfered
    b. transferer
    c. transferable
    d. none of the above

37. *meaning:* "pretending to be what one is not"
    a. hypocrasy
    b. hypocrisy
    c. hypocrosy
    d. none of the above

38. *meaning:* "state of being suspended"
    a. suspenshun
    b. suspensian
    c. suspensiun
    d. none of the above

39. *meaning:* "worth considera-
    tion" (adverb)
    a. considerabley
    b. considerabely
    c. considerably
    d. none of the above

40. past tense of three verbs
    a. shiped
    b. dispeled
    c. equiped
    d. none of the above

41. *ible* or *able*?
    a. partable
    b. negligable
    c. admissible
    d. none of the above

42. *meaning:* "what a doctor
    writes"
    a. prescription
    b. perscription
    c. purscription
    d. none of the above

43. *Check the correct answer.*
    a. corode
    b. coruption
    c. corespond
    d. none of the above

44. *meaning:* "to surpass"
    a. exceed
    b. excede
    c. exsede
    d. none of the above

45. *meaning:* "rapture"
    a. ecstasy
    b. ecstesy
    c. ecstosy
    d. none of the above

46. *meaning:* "to hold steady"
    a. stabalize
    b. stabelize
    c. stabilize
    d. none of the above

47. correct plural
    a. sopranoes
    b. altoes
    c. radioes
    d. none of the above

48. correct plural
    a. potatos
    b. vetos
    c. heroes
    d. none of the above

49. *Check the correct answer.*
    a. transsition
    b. transsom
    c. transsonic
    d. none of the above

50. *meaning:* "wedlock"
    a. marryage
    b. marryed
    c. marrying
    d. none of the above

Answers to Diagnostic Spelling Test

(If you use any part of the book,
you must work your way through the Introduction CAREFULLY.)

Item Number	Correct Answer	Diagnosis—if missed, work Introduction plus:
1	*b*	Chapter 1
2	*b*	Chapter 2
3	*a*	Chapter 11
4	*c*	Chapter 4
5	*a*	Chapter 8
6	*d*	Chapter 11
7	*d*	Chapters 4 and 5
8	*c*	Chapter 11
9	*c*	Chapter 3
10	*d*	Chapters 7 and 10
11	*b*	Chapter 7
12	*c*	Chapter 2
13	*a*	Chapter 8
14	*b*	Chapter 6
15	*c*	Chapter 11
16	*c*	Chapter 3
17	*a*	Chapter 7
18	*d*	Chapter 10
19	*b*	Chapter 5
20	*c*	Chapter 6
21	*b*	Chapter 9
22	*d*	Chapter 9

Item Number	Correct Answer	Diagnosis—if missed, work Introduction plus:
23	*a*	Chapter 10
24	*d*	Chapter 11
25	*b*	Chapter 1
26	*a*	Chapter 3
27	*b*	Chapter 3
28	*a*	Chapter 8
29	*b*	Chapter 8
30	*a*	Chapter 2
31	*b*	Chapter 10
32	*a*	Chapter 7
33	*b*	Chapter 2
34	*c*	Chapter 5
35	*c*	Chapter 4
36	*c*	Chapter 1
37	*b*	Chapter 6
38	*d*	Chapter 7
39	*c*	Chapter 7
40	*d*	Chapter 1
41	*c*	Chapter 11
42	*a*	Chapter 10
43	*d*	Chapter 9
44	*a*	Chapter 8
45	*a*	Chapter 6
46	*c*	Chapter 6
47	*d*	Chapter 5
48	*c*	Chapter 5
49	*d*	Chapter 9
50	*c*	Chapter 4

Introduction

1

Directions: *Cover the answer column with a folded piece of paper.*

A frame is a piece of information plus a blank (_____) in which you write. All this material following the number 1 is a _____.

Check your answer by sliding down your cover paper.

frame

Now go on to frame 2.

2

By checking your answer immediately, you know whether or not you are right. This immediate knowledge helps you to learn only what is _____ (right/wrong).

Check your answer by sliding down your cover paper.

right

Now go on to frame 3.

3

A program is a way of learning that tells you immediately when you are right. When you work a series of frames, certain that you are right, you are learning from a _____.

Check your answer by sliding down your cover paper.

program

4

By means of a program, you can also learn at your own speed. Learning at your own speed and the immediate knowledge that you are learning correctly are both advantages of a _____.

Always check your answers immediately.

program

5

You will learn correct spelling from a program. If you have a spelling class, class will be more interesting because you will come prepared for it, having worked your _____.

Always check your answers immediately.

program *or* assignment

1

6

When you see a plain blank (_____),
your answer will need only one word. In the
sentence, "This is a program to teach čorrect
_____," you know to use
_____ word.

spelling
one

7

This single blank (_____) contains a
clue. It is proportional to the length of the word
needed. This short blank (____) means one
short word. The long blank (_____)
means one _____ word.

long

8

Whenever you see a plain blank space (____
____), you know to write _____ (one/
more than one) word. You also know something
about the _____ (length/com-
plexity) of the word.

one

length

9

Whenever you see a star blank (*_____),
your answer will require more than one word. In
the sentence, "This is a program that teaches *____
_____," your answer
requires *_____.

correct spelling
more than one word

10

In (*_____), there is no clue to the length
of the words or the number of words. The important thing to remember is that (*_____)
means *_____.

more than one word

11

When you see a double-star blank (**_____
____), use your own words. In the sentence, "I
think a program in correct spelling will be
**_____," you are expected
to **_____.

anything you think
use your own words

12

In the sentence, "I want to go to college because (**_____)," you are free to **_____ _____.

use your own words

13

Now summarize what you have learned so far:

(_____) means _____ word.

one

(_____) gives a clue about the _____ of the word.

length

(*_____) means *_____ word.

more than one

(**_____) means **_____ words.

use your own

14

The fact that you check your answer immediately is very important for efficient, accurate learning. Every time you fill a blank, you will **_____ _____.

check the answer immediately

15

When working a program, NEVER LOOK AHEAD. There are many reasons for this, but the important thing to learn now is *_____ _____.

never look ahead

16

You may always look back to find something you have forgotten. You will probably have to look back, but NEVER LOOK _____.

ahead

17

If you make even one error, look back to see where you were wrong. Correct the error; then go on. You may always look _____, but _____ look ahead.

back, never

18

Never let a wrong answer go uncorrected. Each time you make an error, you _____ it.

correct

19

This is a new way of learning. THIS IS NOT A TEST. Remember always, this is a way of _____.

learning

20

Do not be ashamed of a mistake. This is *not* a test. If you make an error, simply look _____ to see where you were wrong and then _____ the error.

back
correct

21

Summarize what you have learned about the mechanics of working a program:

(_____) means _____ word.

one
more than one

(*_____) means *_____ _____ word.

(**_____) means **_____ _____ words.

use your own

22

Remember also:

Any error must be _____.

You may always look _____.

Never look _____.

This is a way of *learning,* not a _____.

corrected
back
ahead
test

23

This program teaches correct spelling by rules and principles. There are a few exceptions to the rules. There could not be exceptions if there were no _____ to which exceptions could be made.

rules

24

The major principle is that **most words are spelled the way they sound.** If you want to spell words correctly, you must learn to listen to their _____.

sounds

25

Every time you spell a word, PRONOUNCE it OUT LOUD and listen to its _____.

sound

26

Pronouncing OUT LOUD is not much good unless you listen to what you are saying. When you spell a word, always pronounce it OUT LOUD and _____ to its sound.

listen

27

This saying and listening to sound will be your biggest help in spelling _____ (how).

correctly

✓
Permission to use this introductory material was kindly granted by John Wiley & Sons, Inc., New York—London—Sydney. It was taken from the introduction to *Medical Terminology: A Programed Text* by Genevieve Love Smith and Dean Phyllis E. Davis.

1   doubling rule

1

This chapter will make you hear accented sounds!
Work with it until you can really hear an accent.

2

Listen to the following two-syllable words and indicate which syllable is accented.

begin _____ (first/second syllable)	second
prefer _____ (first/second syllable)	second
admit _____ (first/second syllable)	second
control _____ (first/second syllable)	second

3

Listen to the following two-syllable words and indicate which syllable is accented.

    —

action _____ (first/second syllable)	first
alien _____ (first/second syllable)	first
alter _____ (first/second syllable)	first
anchor _____ (first/second syllable)	first

4

Listen to the following two-syllable words and indicate which syllable is accented.

program _____ (first/second syllable)	first
compel _____ (first/second syllable)	second
defer _____ (first/second syllable)	second
answer _____ (first/second syllable)	first

5

Listen to the following two-syllable words and indicate which syllable is accented.

deter _____ (first/second syllable)		second
order _____ (first/second syllable)		first
color _____ (first/second syllable)		first
forget _____ (first/second syllable)		second

6

Listen to the following words and hear where the accent occurs.

abnormal _____ (first/second syllable)		second
accustom _____ (first/second syllable)		second
alcohol _____ (first/second syllable)		first
alphabet _____ (first/second syllable)		first

7

The rule for doubling the final consonant depends on hearing the accented syllable. If you are not hearing this, rework the last five frames, pronounce the word aloud, and listen. If you still can't hear the accent, try OVERaccenting one syllable, then the other, e.g., ORder, orDER. This should clear up any difficulty. If necessary, you could have someone pronounce words from a dictionary until you hear correctly. You will not be able to succeed with this chapter until you _____ the accent correctly.

hear

8

Now check to see if you are hearing which syllable is accented.

answerable _____		first
hunger _____		first
confer _____		second
conference _____		first

9

Say and note the accented syllable for:

confer   _____   second
conferred   _____   second
conferring   _____   second
conference _____   first

10

Listen to the words in frame 9. Draw a conclusion. All words accented the _____   second
syllable except the word _____.   conference

11

Listen to the words:

refer
referring
referred
reference

Draw a conclusion. All accents are on the _____   second
_____ syllable except in the word _____.   reference

12

Listen to the words:

prefer
preferred
preferring
preference

Draw a conclusion about the accent. **_____
_____.

Accent was on the second syllable in all words except _prefer-ence,_ where it occurred on the first syllable.

13

Look at the words in frames 9, 11, and 12. After careful examination, can you draw a conclusion about the accent and doubling the final consonant? Try here. **_____
_____.

Compare your conclusion with frame 14.

14

The first part of the doubling rule is, **"Accented last syllable doubles a final consonant before adding a suffix that begins with a vowel."**

15

There is a bit more to this rule than that. Two conditions control it. To understand the controls, review something you learned long ago. The vowels are ___, ___, ___, ___, ___, and sometimes ___ and ___.

a, e, i, o, u, and sometimes *w* and *y*

16

To use the doubling rule, treat *w* and *y* as vowels. For the moment, remember that vowels are ___, ___, ___, ___, ___, and sometimes ___ and ___.

a, e, i, o, u, and sometimes *w* and *y*

17

Also, going way back to grade school, you probably learned that *q* is always followed by ___.

u
Did you remember?

18

Q is followed by *u* to give *q* its own sound. *Qu* is treated as a consonant. Consonants are all letters except the vowels, which are ___, ___, ___, ___, ___, and sometimes ___ and ___.

a, e, i, o, u, and sometimes *w* and *y*

19

In English spelling, *qu* is treated as a ___.

consonant

20

Say the letter *x*. Again — *x*. How many sounds do you hear? ___

two

21

Listen closely to *x*. What are the two sounds you hear? ___ and ___.

ek and *s* or even
k and *s*

22

The *ks* sounds of *x* make *x* a double consonant in both speech and spelling. After all, spelling is built mainly on sound. You must hear _____ as a double consonant.

x

23

In correct speech and spelling, *qu* is a _____ (vowel/consonant), *x* is a *_____, and all other letters are consonants except ___, ___, ___, ___, ___, and sometimes ___ and ___.

consonant
double consonant
a, e, i, o, u, and sometimes *w* and *y*

24

Examine the next page. Study *all of it* before starting to use it in working as many of the remaining frames as you *need* to.

Go to next page.

DOUBLE FINAL CONSONANT WHEN:

The word is a one-syllable word (*get*);

or

the accent occurs on the last syllable of the word (*ad mit'*) or word root (*me tal' lic*).

ONLY UNDER THE FOLLOWING CONTROLLING CONDITIONS:

1. The word ends in a final *single* consonant preceded by a *single* vowel.

2. The suffix begins with a vowel.

drip   one-syllable word
p single consonant ending
i single preceding vowel
ing suffix beginning with a vowel
word—*dripping*

a bet'   accented final syllable
t single consonant ending
e single preceding vowel
er suffix beginning with a vowel
word—*abetter*

e quip'   accented final syllable
p single consonant ending
i single preceding vowel (*qu* is a consonant—*Remember?*)
ed suffix beginning with a vowel
word—*equipped*
BUT equip*m*ent

25

To the word *abhor,* add the following suffixes:

er	abhorrer
ence	abhorrence
ent	abhorrent
ing	abhorring

26

To the word *commit,* add the following suffixes:

ing	committing
able	committable
al	committal
ment	commitment

27

To the word *drug,* add the following:

ed	drugged
ing	drugging
ist	druggist
store	drugstore

28

Do what is necessary to form complete words from the indicated parts:

abet	+ ing	abetting
adapt	+ ed	adapted
absurd	+ ity	absurdity
alcohol	+ ism	alcoholism

Listen and think!

29

While *pronouncing, listening,* and *thinking,* form correct words from the indicated parts:

foot	+ er	footer
accident	+ al	accidental
hunger	+ ed	hungered
adorn	+ ment	adornment

30

Continue building and spelling words correctly from parts.

order + ed	_____	ordered
order + ly	_____	orderly
deter + ing	_____	deterring
deter + ment	_____	determent

31

Continue building and spelling words correctly from parts.

rid + ance	_____	riddance
acquit + al	_____	acquittal *(frame 18)*
flex + ion	_____	flexion *(frame 22)*
acquaint + ance	_____	acquaintance

32

Continue building and spelling words correctly from parts.

borrow + er	_____	borrower
basic + ally	_____	basically
accord + ing	_____	according
accustom + ed	_____	accustomed

Listen!

33

Continue building and spelling words correctly from parts.

fog + ed	_____	fogged
fog + y	_____	foggy *(frame 16)*
anchor + age	_____	anchorage
stow + age	_____	stowage *(frame 16)*

34

Continue building and spelling words correctly from parts.

box + ing	_____	boxing
throw + ing	_____	throwing
control + ing	_____	controlling
program + ing	_____	programing
sound + ing	_____	sounding
abstain + ing	_____	abstaining

35

Are you still referring to page 11? Try working this frame without it.

expel + ed _____	expell'ed
answer + ed _____	an'swered
adapt + ed _____	ada*p*ted
flex + ed _____	fle*x*ed
avoid + ed _____	av*oi*ded
allow + ed _____	allo*w*ed

36

Without looking at page 11, build and spell words from these parts:

allot + ed _____	allotted
allot + ment _____	allotment
assort + ed _____	assorted
assort + ment _____	assortment

37

Without page 11, build and spell words from these parts:

attain + ed _____	attained
attain + ment _____	attainment
endow + ed _____	endowed
endow + ment _____	endowment
fix + ed _____	fixed

38

Build and spell words from these parts: (*Listen for changes of accent!*)

prefer + ed _____	preferred (pre fer' red)
prefer + ment _____	preferment (pre fer' ment)
prefer + ence _____	preference (pref' er ence)
prefer + able _____	preferable (pref' er able)

39

Did you hear the change of accent in frame 38? Try again while building words from:

confer + ing   _____

confer + ed   _____

confer + ment _____

confer + ence _____

conferring
(con fer′ ring)
conferred
(con ferred′)
conferment
(con fer′ ment)
conference
(con′ fer ence)

40

Watch for accent changes while building words from:

infer + ed   _____
infer + ing   _____
infer + ence _____

inferred
inferring
inference

41

One more change-of-accent frame before the big check. Build and spell words correctly from:

defer + ed   _____
defer + ence _____
defer + ment _____
defer + ing   _____

deferred
deference
deferment
deferring

42
Self-test

In Column II, write the correct word. Next, check your answers at the bottom of the page. Correct any mistakes in Column II. Write your correct answer in Column III.

Column I	Column II	Column III
1. ship + ed		
2. admit + ance		
3. alien + ate		
4. account + ant		
5. equip + ing		
6. act + ion		
7. apt + ness		
8. cartoon + ist		
9. acclaim + ed		
10. brew + er		
11. fix + ation		
12. dispel + ing		
13. allot + ment		
14. erect + ly		
15. cat + y		

1. shipped	6. action	11. fixation
2. admittance	7. aptness	12. dispelling
3. alienate	8. cartoonist	13. allotment
4. accountant	9. acclaimed	14. erectly
5. equipping	10. brewer	15. catty

43

As with nearly all of our rules, there are exceptions. When you think about all of the languages from which English borrows words, there are really very few exceptions.

Browse through your dictionary sometime to see the many languages that have contributed to English.

44

Study the words:

    crystal
    crystalling
    crystallite
    crystalloid

Words built from *crystal* plus a suffix that begins with a vowel are exceptions to the doubling rule because **_____.

Accent is on first syllable, but the *l* is doubled.

45

Remember, *crystal* words are exceptions. They keep the doubling rule from being *crystal clear*. The first exceptions to the rule are words built with

_____.

crystal

46

Study the following words:

    transfer
    transferring
    transferred
    transferrer
    transferable

The word that is an exception to the doubling rule is

transferable

47

Transferable is an exception to the doubling rule because **_____.

The accent stays on *fer,* but the *r* is not doubled.

48

The lack of *crystal* clarity is *transferable* to other words in the _____ rule.

doubling

49

This lack of *crystal* clarity is *transferable* to four words with a French involvement. They are *chagrin, legionnaire, questionnaire,* and *ricochet.*

50

You are safe with *ricochet* because it follows the rule. It all depends on how you say it.

If you say the French *rik o sha',* spell this way:	If you say the English *rik o shet',* spell this way:
ricocheted (rik o shād)	ricochetted (rik o shĕt' id)
ricocheting (rik o shā' ing)	ricochetting (rik o shĕt ing)

Write the French form several times. (This is the most used.)

_____ _____

_____ _____

_____ _____

51

I am chagrined to present you with another French word. *Chagrin'* is accented on the last syllable, ends in a single consonant preceded by a single vowel, but does *not* double the *n.* Build the words:

chagrin + ed _____

chagrin + ing _____

chagrined
chagrining

52

I am *chagrined* at the lack of *crystal* clarity in the doubling rule which is *transferable* to two more words. When taking the French suffix *aire, legion* and *question* do double. Write them here:

_____   _____
_____   _____
_____   _____

legionnaire
questionnaire

53

Legionnaire and questionnaire are exceptions to the doubling rule because **_____
_____.

The final consonant is doubled even though it is preceded by two vowels and the words accent the first syllable.

54

Remember to feel *chagrined* at the lack of *crystal* clarity in the doubling rule which is *transferable* to *legionnaire* and *questionnaire*.

55

A bonus for you—something extra thrown in: **Words that end in a double consonant keep both consonants.** Build words from:

excess + ive   _____   excessive
skill   + ful   _____   skillful
dull   + ness   _____   dullness
discuss + ing   _____   discussing

56

To round off your bonus, build words from:

odd + ish   _____   oddish
stiff + ness   _____   stiffness
ebb + ing   _____   ebbing
will + ful   _____   willful

A Summary of Exceptions to the Doubling Rule

crystal words
transferable
chagrined
legionnaire
questionnaire

plus

personnel
chancellor
pistillate

(*This is really specialized vocabulary. You may not need to know it. Check with your dictionary, then learn it if you are likely to use it.*)

USE WHAT YOU HAVE LEARNED

What you have learned is only yours so long as you use it. Even if you are not confident about this rule, USE IT. Then look up the word in the dictionary.

2   final silent *e* before a suffix

1

You are improving your spelling by learning to hear sounds and by learning some rules and principles that involve the correct **_____ of sounds.

         hearing

2

There are a few things you can learn about sounds that will help you with spelling. *C* and *g* before *a* and *o* have a hard sound. Hear the hard sound of *c* in the word *cat*. Hear the _____ sound of *c* in the word *cot*.

         hard

3

Hear the hard sound of *c* in the word *came*. Hear the _____ sound of *c* in the word *come*.

         hard

4

The sound of *c* in the word *cap* is a _____ sound.

         hard

The sound of *c* in the word *cop* is a _____ sound.

         hard

The sound of *g* in the word *gap* is a _____ sound.

         hard

The sound of *g* in the word *got* is a _____ sound.

         hard

5

The sound of *g* in the word *game* is a _____ sound.

         hard

The sound of *g* in the word *gone* is a _____ sound.

         hard

The sound of *g* in the word *gather* is a _____ sound.

         hard

The sound of *c* in the word *community* is a _____ sound.

         hard

6

To contrast with this hard sound of *c* and *g* before
a and *o*, *c* and *g* usually have a soft sound before
e and *i*. Hear the soft sound of *c* in the word *cent*.
Hear the _____ sound of *g* in the word
gentle.

soft

7

Hear the soft sound of *c* in the word *cereal*.

The sound of *g* in the word *generous* is a _____
sound.

soft

The sound of *c* in the word *cinema* is a _____
sound.

soft

The sound of *g* in the word *giant* is a _____
sound.

soft

8

The sound of *c* in the word *cigarette* is a _____
sound.

soft

The sound of *g* in the word *ginger* is a _____
sound.

soft

The sound of *c* in the word *cell* is a _____
sound.

soft

The sound of *g* in the word *general* is a _____
sound.

soft

9

The sound of *c* in the word *carpet* is a _____
sound.

hard

The sound of *c* in the word *carrot* is a _____
sound.

hard

The sound of *c* in the word *certain* is a _____
sound.

soft

The sound of *c* in the word *casual* is a _____
sound.

hard

Listen!

10

The sound of *g* in the word *good* is a _____ sound.

hard

The sound of *g* in the word *genius* is a _____ sound.

soft

The sound of *g* in the word *geometry* is a _____ sound.

soft

The sound of *g* in the word *gambler* is a _____ sound.

hard

11

Summarize the principle you have used in working the last nine frames. "**_____ _____."

C and *g* are hard sounds before *a* and *o*, and soft sounds before *e* and *i*.

12

It also helps with spelling to know how words are formed. You will still have to **_____ sounds correctly.

hear *or* listen to

13

Every word has a word root. This is the basic building block from which a word is built. Sometimes the word root is a word in itself. *Port* is a word, but it is also a *_____.

word root

14

Often a word is a word root. *Form* is a word, but it is also a *_____.

word root

15

Fix is a word, but it is also a *_____.

word root

16

In the words *im/plant*, *trans/plant*, and *sup/plant*, the word root is _____.

plant

17

In the words *plant/er*, *plant/able*, and *plant/ation*, the word root is _____.

plant

18

Look at frame 16. We have changed the meaning of *plant* by putting _____, _____, and _____ before it.

im
trans
sup

19

Look at frame 17. We have changed the meaning of *plant* by putting _____, _____, and _____ after it.

er
able
ation

20

In both frames 16 and 17, we have changed the meaning of *plant* by adding something to it. In both frames, *plant* is the building block of different words. This means that in these frames *plant* is the *_____.

word root

21

A prefix is what we put before a word root to change its meaning. In the words *pre/fix*, *af/fix*, *suf/fix*, and *trans/fix*, *pre*, *af*, *suf*, and *trans* are _____es.

prefix(es)

22

Pre is a prefix meaning "before." In the words *im/port*, *trans/port*, and *sup/port*, *im*, *trans*, and *sup* are _____es.

prefix(es)

23

In the words *im/plant*, *trans/plant*, and *sup/plant*, *im*, *trans*, and *sup* are the _____es.

prefix (es)

24

In the words *in/form*, *re/form*, and *trans/form*, the prefixes are _____, _____, and _____.

in
re
trans

25

Look at frame 24. *Form* is the *_____.

word root

26

A suffix is what we put after a word root to change its meaning. In the words *port/er, port/able,* and *port/age, er, able,* and *age* are _____es.

suffix (es)

27

Even *ing* in *plant/ing* is a suffix. In the words *plant/er, plant/able,* and *plant/ation, er, able,* and *ation* are _____es.

suffix (es)

28

In the words *fix/able, fix/ative,* and *fix/ation, able, ative,* and *ation* are _____es.

suffix (es)

29

In the words *form/able, form/ative,* and *form/ation,* the suffixes are _____, _____, and _____.

able
ative
ation

30

Look at frame 29. The words built in this frame have *form* as the *_____.

word root

31

The main part of the word is the *_____. We change the meaning of a word by putting a _____ before it or a _____ after it.

word root
prefix
suffix

32

Now you can learn some rules of spelling that relate to suffixes. One rule that is simple and applies to many words is the rule of the final silent *e* before adding a suffix.

Go to next frame.

33

Drop the final silent *e* when adding a suffix that begins with a vowel. A word from *love* + *able* is *lovable*. A word from *advise* + *able* is

_____.

advisable

34

To spell *desirable* from *desire* + *able*, we drop the final silent *e* from *desire* because *able* begins with a vowel. A word from *value* + *able* is _____.

valuable

35

Build a word from:

improve	+ able	improvable
use	+ able	usable
advise	+ able	advisable
sense	+ ible	sensible

36

Build a word from:

force	+ ible	forcible
like	+ able	likable
desire	+ ous	desirous
serve	+ ice	service

37

Build a word from:

come	+ ing	coming
sterile	+ ize	sterilize
love	+ er	lover
interfere	+ ence	interference

38

Build a word from:

tense	+ ion	tension
slave	+ ery	slavery
animate	+ ed	animated
care	+ ing	caring

39

State what rule you have been using to build the words in the last four frames. "**_____
_____."

Drop final silent *e* when adding a suffix that begins with a vowel.

40

There are *two exceptions* to the rule, "Drop the final silent *e* from a word before adding suffixes that begin with a vowel." The *first exception* is: **"Retain the final silent *e* to keep the *soft* sound of *c* or *g* before *o* or *a*."**

Continue to pronounce even simple words aloud.

41

Indicate in the following words whether the sound of *c* or *g* before *able* is a hard/soft sound:

changeable _____	soft
navigable _____	hard
despicable _____	hard
serviceable _____	soft

Pronounce them again and listen!

42

Build a word from:

peace + able _____	peaceable
charge + able _____	chargeable
trace + able _____	traceable
manage + able _____	manageable

43

Build a word from:

practice + able _____ ("able to be practiced")	practiceable
practice + able _____ ("feasible," "practical")	practicable (hard *c*)
notice + able _____	noticeable
marriage + able _____	marriageable
knowledge + able _____	knowledgeable

44

The sound of *c* or *g* before *ous* is a _____
(hard/soft) sound. If you followed the rule and
dropped the *e* from courage before adding *ous* you
would be saying a different word. Pronounce and
listen to:

      couragous (hard *g*) and
      courageous (soft *g*).

Obviously _____ is
correct.

hard

courageous

45

Build a word from:

    outrage   + ous _____
    gorge   + ous _____
    advantage + ous _____

outrageous
gorgeous
advantageous

46

Words ending with *ce* USUALLY change the *e* to
i before the ending *ous*. When this happens, the *ci*
has a *sh* sound. Pronounce *gracious*. This sound of
c is _____ (hard/soft). In *gracious* the
ci has a _____ (*ch/ss/sh/sz*) sound.

soft
sh

47

Build a word from:

    malice   + ous _____
    space   + ous _____
    avarice + ous _____
    auspice + ous _____

malicious
spacious
avaricious
auspicious

48

Complete the rule. Drop the final silent *e* from a
word before suffixes beginning with a _____.

vowel

49

An exception to the above rule of final silent *e*:
"Retain final silent *e* to keep the _____
(hard/soft) sound of *c* or *g* before suffixes beginning with _____ or _____."

soft

a or *o*

50

The *next exception* to the rule about dropping final silent *e* is a mixed-up one. It involves either correct sound or avoiding confusion with other words. There are two ways of learning the seven words that are exceptions. One is by analyzing and understanding them. The other is by a simple memory gimmick. Choose the method that suits you best.

Method I

1. Keep the *e* in *singeing* to retain the *j* sound and to avoid confusion with the word *singing*.

2. When changing the color of something, use *dyeing* to avoid confusion with *dying*.

3. In *shoeing* and *hoeing* and *toeing*, keep the *e* between the *o* and *i*. *Oi* is pronounced *oy*.

4. The word *acreage* is pronounced *a' ker ij*, not *ak rage*.

5. Keep the *e* in *mileage* to avoid confusion with *millage* (a rate of taxation).

Method II

When singeing my hair,
When dyeing my shoes,
When shoeing my horse,
When hoeing my corn,
When toeing the mark,
I keep the *e*—
Even with mileage and acreage.

51

Refer to your chosen method, *if necessary*, to spell the words correctly in the next eight frames. SAY. HEAR. THINK!

52

The blond was (dye + ing) _____   dyeing
her hair red.

He started to run the mile by (toe + ing)
_____ the mark.   toeing

The boat was (tow + ing) _____   towing
the barge.

53

The boy was (shoe + ing) _____   shoeing
his horse before (show + ing) _____   showing
it in the ring.

54

I thought I had (acre + age) _____,   acreage
but it seemed like (mile + age) _____   mileage
after (hoe + ing) _____ my corn.   hoeing

55

In the dressing room at the last minute, the girl
was (singe + ing) _____ her hair   singeing
before (sing + ing) _____ her solo   singing
on stage.

56

Before (dye + ing) _____ the   dyeing
leather, he was (singe + ing) _____   singeing
it in spots to give a more interesting texture.

57

She is (die + ing) _____ to know   dying
my secret for (dye + ing) _____   dyeing
my hair.

58

The guard was (toe + ing) _____   toeing
the 40-yard mark when the referee blew his
whistle.

59

While (hoe + ing) _____ my   hoeing
(acre + age) _____, I thought of   acreage
(shoe + ing) _____ my horse be-   shoeing
fore turning him out to cover great (mile + age)
_____.   mileage

60
Self-test

In Column II, write the correct word. Next, check your answers at the bottom of the page. Correct any mistakes in Column II. Write your correct answer in Column III.

Column I	Column II	Column III
1. ridicule + ous		
2. abdicate + ing		
3. abuse + ive		
4. agitate + ion		
5. courage + ous		
6. desire + ous		
7. acquire + ing		
8. dye + ing		
9. virtue + ous		
10. outrage + ous		
11. mile + age		
12. agitate + or		
13. advance + ing		
14. shoe + ing		
15. negate + ion		
16. advantage + ous		
17. abbreviate + ion		
18. toe + ing		
19. abuse + ing		
20. singe + ing		

1. ridiculous
2. abdicating
3. abusive
4. agitation
5. courageous
6. desirous
7. acquiring
8. dyeing
9. virtuous
10. outrageous
11. mileage
12. agitator
13. advancing
14. shoeing
15. negation
16. advantageous
17. abbreviation
18. toeing
19. abusing
20. singeing

61

The *rule* (no exceptions wanted) that you have now learned about final silent *e* is, "**_____

_____."

Drop the final silent *e* from a word before adding a suffix that begins with a vowel.

62

There is one other rule about final silent *e*: **"Keep final silent *e* before adding suffixes that begin with a consonant."**

achieve + ment is spelled _____	achievement
acute + ness is spelled _____	acuteness

63

agile + ly is spelled agilely	
lithe + some is spelled _____	lithesome
acquire + ment is spelled _____	acquirement

64

advance + ment is spelled _____	advancement
aware + ness is spelled _____	awareness
accurate + ly is spelled _____	accurately
trouble + some is spelled _____	troublesome

65

Take the word *advise* and change its meaning by adding the indicated suffixes correctly.

ed _____	advised
ment _____	advisement
ing _____	advising
er _____	adviser

66

With the word *appraise,* change its meaning by adding the indicated suffixes correctly.

al _____	appraisal
er _____	appraiser
ing _____	appraising
ment _____	appraisement

67

Using the word *battle,* add the indicated word parts correctly.

ing	battling
ment	battlement
er	battler
ship	battleship
ed	battled
ground	battleground
field	battlefield

68

When you formed the word _____ from *appraise* + *ment,* you were using the rule, "Keep the final silent *e* before adding suffixes that begin **_____."

appraisement

with a consonant

69

When you used *acute* + *ness* to form the word _____, you used the rule, "Keep the final silent *e* before adding **_____ ."

acuteness
suffixes that begin with a consonant

70

When you took *accurate* + *ly* to form the word _____, you used the rule, "**_____ ."

accurately
Keep the final silent *e* before adding suffixes that begin with a consonant.

71

There are two *exceptions* to the rule, "Keep the final silent *e* before adding suffixes that begin with a consonant." Both exceptions are easy.

72

One exception to the rule of keeping final silent *e* occurs in words that end in the long sound of *u.* Hear the sound of *u* in the word *hue.* It is the *long* sound of *u.* The sound of *u* in the word *true* is the _____ sound of *u.*

long
Listen!

73

The word *argue* has the long sound of *u*.

The word *virtue* has the _____ sound of *u*.

long

The word *due* has the _____ sound of *u*.

long

The word *blue* has the _____ sound of *u*.

long

Did you say them aloud?

74

When the word ends in the long sound of *u*, drop the silent *e* before adding suffixes. (EXCEPTIONS: *blueness, trueness, accruement, gluey, rueful*) Compound words (two words) don't count. (EXAMPLES: *bluefish* and *trueborn*) Learn only the *u* exceptions that you need to know or don't already know. Work out your own memory device.

75

When the word ends in the long sound of *u*, drop the silent *e* before adding suffixes.

hue + ed becomes hued
true + ly becomes _____

truly

76

due   + ly   becomes _____

duly

sue   + ing becomes _____

suing

queue + ed   becomes _____

queued

virtue + al   becomes _____

virtual

77

When you took *argue* + *ment* to form _____
_____, you used the exception, "When the word ends in the long sound of *u*, **_____
_____."

argument
drop the silent *e* before adding a suffix

78

When you used *true* + *ism* to form the word
_____, you used the exception, "**_____
_____."

truism
When the word ends in the long sound of *u*, drop the silent *e* before adding a suffix.

79

Words That Are Exceptions to "Keep *the Final
Silent e When Adding Suffixes That Begin
with a Consonant.*"

Say aloud and hear the *dj* sound in the words
*acknowle***d**ge, *abri***d**ge, and *ju***d**ge. Repeat this,
saying and listening to the *dj* sound.

To add *ment,* drop the *e.*

judg∉ment   abridg∉ment   acknowledg∉ment

Say and listen to the above three words several
times. Write them correctly here:

_____   _____   _____
_____   _____   _____
_____   _____   _____

80

Exceptions continued

There are three odd-ball words that drop the *e*
when adding suffixes that begin with a consonant. Let's play baseball.

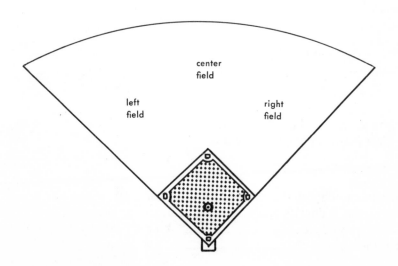

One odd ball for left field.

> The left fielder is usually waiting for the *ninth* inning.

One odd ball for right field.

> The right fielder must be *wholly* keen when playing a ball to the infield.

One odd ball for center field.

> The center fielder must use baseball *wisdom* to cover such a large area.

81

judge + ment	is spelled _____	judgment
nine + th	is spelled _____	ninth
whole + ly	is spelled _____	wholly

82

acknowledge + ment	is spelled _____	acknowledgment
wise + dom	is spelled _____	wisdom
abridge + ment	is spelled _____	abridgment
whole + ly	is spelled _____	wholly

83

The center fielder must use baseball (wise + dom) _____ to cover such a large area.

wisdom

84

The left fielder is usually waiting for the (nine + th) _____ inning.

ninth

85

The right fielder must be (whole + ly) _____ keen when playing a ball to the infield.

wholly

86

For the three odd balls, a baseball player must have the (wise + dom) _____ to be (whole + ly) _____ keen through the (nine + th) _____ inning.

wisdom
wholly
ninth

87

We should use good (judge + ment) _____
_____ when driving a car.

judgment

88

She wrote an (acknowledge + ment) _____
_____ of the order.

acknowledgment

89

This book is an (abridge + ment) _____
_____ of the original publication.

abridgment

90

This sentence is *not* a model of proper construction!

The first base umpire was not whol____ keen
when he lacked the wis____ to see that he
was creating an abridg_____ of the rules
when he reversed his judg_____ (without
the acknowledg_____ of the other umpires) in the nin____ inning.

wholly
wisdom
abridgment
judgment
acknowledgment
ninth

91

In frame 90, the words used are exceptions to the
rule, "**_____
_____."

Keep the final silent *e*
when adding a suffix
that begins with a consonant.

92
Self-test

In Column II, write the correct word. Next, check your answers at the bottom of the page. Correct any mistakes in Column II. Write your correct answer in Column III.

Column I	Column II	Column III
1. love + able		
2. true + ly		
3. courage + ous		
4. achieve + ment		
5. dye + ing		
6. care + ing		
7. abridge + ment		
8. acute + ness		
9. acknowledge + ment		
10. toe + ing		
11. desire + ous		
12. shoe + ing		
13. battle + er		
14. wise + dom		
15. outrage + ous		
16. acre + age		
17. serve + ice		
18. whole + ly		
19. aware + ness		
20. argue + ment		
21. advantage + ous		
22. judge + ment		
23. slave + ery		
24. singe + ing		
25. nine + th		

1. lovable	9. acknowledgment	17. service
2. truly	10. toeing	18. wholly
3. courageous	11. desirous	19. awareness
4. achievement	12. shoeing	20. argument
5. dyeing	13. battler	21. advantageous
6. caring	14. wisdom	22. judgment
7. abridgment	15. outrageous	23. slavery
8. acuteness	16. acreage	24. singeing
		25. ninth

93

A bonus for you—maybe. This is so easy that you probably don't need it. If you do, here it is: *ie* **in an accented syllable becomes** *y* **before a suffix beginning with** *i.*

Examples:
   die–dying
   tie–tying
   lie–lying

94

Add the suffix *ing* to the following:

vie	vying
hie	hying
untie	untying
belie	belying

You noticed that the *e* was a silent *e*, didn't you? Pronounce and listen to the sound if you didn't.

USE WHAT YOU HAVE LEARNED

What you have learned is only yours so long as you use it. Even if you are not confident about this rule, USE IT. *Then* look up the word in the dictionary.

3   ie/ei

1

Four useful rules of correct spelling concern the sounds of *e* in words which contain *ie* or *ei*. *Remember,* if you want to spell correctly, you must pronounce it correctly and **＊＊_____ the sound you pronounce.

hear *or* listen to

2

The first sound of *e* that you will learn is the sound of *e* in the word *me*. People are really most interested in themselves, so you will learn the sound of *e* in the word _____.

me

Did you say it aloud, listen to it, and look at what you wrote?

3

The sound of *e* in the word *me* is the long sound of *e*. The sound of *e* in the word *be* is the _____ sound of *e*.

long

4

The sound of *e* in the word *see* is the long sound of *e*. The sound of *ie* in the word *believe* is the _____ sound of *e*.

long

5

The sound of *ie* in the word *piece* is the _____ sound of *e*. The sound of *ei* in the word *conceit* is the _____ sound of *e*.

long

long

6

The rule for using *ei* and *ie* when they have the long sound of *e* is, *"i before e except after c."* This rule applies to words with the _____ sound of *e*.

long

7

"I before e except after c" is the rule for spelling words that contain an *ie* or *ei* combination and have the long sound of e. In spelling the word *brief,* you have used the rule, "**_____ _____.*"

i before *e* except after *c*

8

In spelling the word *grief,* you have used the rule, "**_____."

i before *e* except after *c*

9

In spelling the word *deceive,* you have used the rule, "**_____."

i before *e* except after *c*

10

The rule, *"i before e except after c,"* applies to words with the _____ sound of *e*.

long

11
Self-test

In Column I, fill the blank with either *ie* or *ei*. Next, check your answer at the bottom of the page. Correct any mistakes in Column I. Write the correct word twice; once in Column II, once in Column III. Pronounce the word you are spelling.

Column I	Column II	Column III
1. br____f	_____	_____
2. bel____ve	_____	_____
3. gr____f	_____	_____
4. conc____ve	_____	_____
5. dec____t	_____	_____
6. pr____st	_____	_____
7. c____ling	_____	_____
8. n____ce	_____	_____
9. prair____	_____	_____
10. perc____ve	_____	_____
11. rec____pt	_____	_____
12. th____f	_____	_____
13. f____nd	_____	_____
14. conc____t	_____	_____
15. rec____ve	_____	_____
16. hyg____ne	_____	_____
17. dec____ve	_____	_____

1. brief	7. ceiling	13. fiend
2. believe	8. niece	14. conceit
3. grief	9. prairie	15. receive
4. conceive	10. perceive	16. hygiene
5. deceit	11. receipt	17. deceive
6. priest	12. thief	

12

The rule that you have been using says, "___ before ___ except after ___" when the sound of *e* is
_____.

i

e, c

long

13

There are seven words that have the long sound of
e and do not follow this rule. Six *of* these words
have a long *e* sound, do not follow *c*, and use the
ei combination. They are e*i*ther, ne*i*ther, le*i*sure,
we*i*rd, se*i*ze, and she*i*k. Read the following:

The she*i*k se*i*zed a le*i*sure distinguished,
Though his tribe thought him we*i*rd to learn
         English.
He learned e*i*ther-or,
Also ne*i*ther-nor,
         to's
But three too's his ambition extinguished.
         two's

Can you write a verse, limerick or catch phrase
using these six *ei* words? Try for ten minutes. There
is room on this page.

After ten minutes, go to the next page.

I'll bet you can top this one!

> *Ei*ther s*ei*ze the sh*ei*k at his l*ei*sure,
> or n*ei*ther w*ei*rd chants nor wild music
> will aid in his capture.

How do you compare with this one?

> There was a young sh*ei*k, an Iraqi,
> Who was a wild, w*ei*rd, hep disc jockey.
> With n*ei*ther sleep nor l*ei*sure
> He suffered a s*ei*zure,
> Which *ei*ther meant rest or be rocky.

Use yours or any of these, but one of them should help you remember the six words that have the long sound of *e*, do not follow *c*, and still take *ei*.

(**Caution:** This rule is not intended to apply to technical words. EXAMPLES: *olein, protein, pleiades.*)

14
Or is used with _____ther. *Nor* is used with _____.

ei
neither

15
The witch's chant sounded like a w_____rd cry. In fact, it sounded _____ly all night long.

ei
weird

16
The sh_____k was subject to epileptic s_____zures. Fortunately, his _____ were of short duration.

ei, ei
seizures

17
The runaway sh_____k rode a snow white horse across the desert during the night. The father of the _____ pursued him on a black horse.

ei

sheik

18

I need some l____sure time for reading. In fact, I
need much more _____ time
for reading.

ei

leisure

19
Self-test

In Column I, fill the blank with either *ie* or *ei*. Next, check your answer at the
bottom of the page. Correct any mistakes in Column I. Write the correct word
twice; once in Column II, once in Column IIi. Pronounce the word you are spelling.

Column I	Column II	Column III
1. f____nd	_____	_____
2. fift____s	_____	_____
3. dec____ved	_____	_____
4. s____ze	_____	_____
5. rel____ve	_____	_____
6. s____ge	_____	_____
7. gr____ve	_____	_____
8. gr____vance	_____	_____
9. apperc____ve	_____	_____
10. p____ce	_____	_____
11. w____rd	_____	_____
12. l____surely	_____	_____
13. rec____ved	_____	_____
14. conc____vable	_____	_____
15. n____ther	_____	_____

1. fiend	6. siege	11. weird
2. fifties	7. grieve	12. leisurely
3. deceived	8. grievance	13. received
4. seize	9. apperceive	14. conceivable
5. relieve	10. piece	15. neither

20

There is only one other word which is an exception to the long sound of *e-ei/ie* rule. It is *financier.* Relate it to the word *financial.* Pronounce **financial** correctly, and you can't miss it: fi nan′ ci al.

> financ___r
> financial

Also: A financier is a good friend to have.

ie

21

The second rule involving *ie* has one exception. **If the vowel combination is involved with the sound of *sh* or *ch,* it occurs always as *ie*** (except *sheik*). Hear the sound of *ch* in the word **cheese.** Hear the sound of *sh* in the word **sheet.**

22

In the word *cherry,* you can hear the sound *ch.*
In the word *cheer,* the first sound is _____.
In the word *sherry,* the initial sound is *sh.*
In the word *sheer,* the initial sound is _____.

ch

sh

23

Choose and **ch**ip start with the sound _____.
Shoes and **sh**ip begin with the sound _____.

ch
sh

24

Chief and *ancient* both contain the sound _____.
Shield and *deficient* both contain the sound ____.

ch
sh

25

Look at the words in frame 24—*chief, ancient, shield, deficient.* Pronounce them. LISTEN. HEAR. The vowel combination of *i* and *e* is _____ if it is involved with a *sh* sound or *ch* sound.

ie

26

Pronounce *sufficient* and *deficient.* Spell suffic___ntly and defic___ncy.

ie
ie

27

Say *chief* and *patient*. Spell ch____ftain and pat____ntly.

ie
ie

28
Self-test

In Column I, fill the blank with either *ie* or *ei*. Next, check your answer at the bottom of the page. Correct any mistakes in Column I. Write the correct word twice; once in Column II, once in Column III. Pronounce the word you are spelling.

Column I	Column II	Column III
1. consc____nce	_____	_____
2. pat____nt	_____	_____
3. defic____nt	_____	_____
4. anc____nt	_____	_____
5. suffic____t	_____	_____
6. effic____nt	_____	_____
7. profic____nt	_____	_____
8. ach____ve	_____	_____
9. ch____f	_____	_____
10. spec____ (spe′ shēz)	_____	_____
11. sh____ld	_____	_____
12. consc____ntious	_____	_____
13. spec____ (spē′ shē)	_____	_____
14. insuffic____nt	_____	_____
15. defic____ncy	_____	_____
16. ch____fly	_____	_____
17. impat____ntly	_____	_____
18. sh____lded	_____	_____

Should you look up the meanings of spec*ie* and spec*ie*s in your dictionary?

1. conscience	7. proficient	13. specie
2. patient	8. achieve	14. insufficient
3. deficient	9. chief	15. deficiency
4. ancient	10. species	16. chiefly
5. sufficient	11. shield	17. impatiently
6. efficient	12. conscientious	18. shielded

29

Isn't that an easy rule? The main thing is to hear *sh* and *ch* sounds, then use ———— (*ei/ie*).

ie

30

When you have a combination of *ie* or *ei* with the long sound of *e,* you use ———— except after *c,* then use ————.

ie
ei

31

There are six *ei* and one *ie* exceptions to the rule in frame 30. The *ei* exceptions occur in the words,

——————, ——————, ——————, ——————, ——————, ——————.

either, neither, sheik, seize, leisure, weird

32

The *ie* exception to the rule of long sound of *e* is *financier.* One way to remember *financier* is to connect it to *financial.* Remember that a financ——r is a good fr*ie*nd to have.

ie

33

A financ——r is a good fr*ie*nd to have. A —————————— is an expert on financial matters.

ie
financier

34

If you are spelling a word in which the sounds *sh* or *ch* influence an *ie/ei* combination, use ————.

ie

35
Self-test

In Column I, fill the blank with either *ie* or *ei*. Next, check your answer at the bottom of the page. Correct any mistakes in Column I. Write the correct word twice; once in Column II, once in Column III. Pronounce the word you are spelling.

Column I	Column II	Column III
1. sixt____s	_____	_____
2. c____lings	_____	_____
3. l____n	_____	_____
4. rec____pt	_____	_____
5. p____rce	_____	_____
6. ach____ve	_____	_____
7. sh____k	_____	_____
8. conc____ted	_____	_____
9. w____rd	_____	_____
10. effic____nt	_____	_____
11. defic____nt	_____	_____
12. financ____r	_____	_____
13. f____rce	_____	_____
14. repr____ve	_____	_____
15. dec____ve	_____	_____
16. n____ther	_____	_____
17. pat____nce	_____	_____
18. consc____nce	_____	_____
19. conc____ve	_____	_____
20. l____sure	_____	_____

1. sixt*ie*s	8. conc*ei*ted	15. dec*ei*ve
2. c*ei*lings	9. w*ei*rd	16. n*ei*ther
3. l*ie*n	10. effic*ie*nt	17. pat*ie*nce
4. rec*ei*pt	11. defic*ie*nt	18. consc*ie*nce
5. p*ie*rce	12. financ*ie*r	19. conc*ei*ve
6. ach*ie*ve	13. f*ie*rce	20. l*ei*sure
7. sh*ei*k	14. repr*ie*ve	

36

These *ie*'s and *ei*'s are becoming pretty easy, aren't they? Listen to the following words as you pronounce them aloud: *quiet, gaiety, audience, science, experience, thirtieth, twentieth, variety.* Can you draw a conclusion from what you hear? If so, write it here. **_____.

The sound of *ie* is a split sound, or double sound.

37

If you missed frame 36, or even just for fun, listen to these words for the split sound of *ie: diet, orient, alien, fortieth, piety, obedient, soviet,* and *brier.*

Did you hear the split sound?

38

In hearing the words in frames 36 and 37, you heard many sounds. One thing that you heard in each word was that the sound of *ie* was a _____ _____ sound.

split *or* double

39

Look at the words in frames 36 and 37. Can you see a rule about the occurrence of *ie* or *ei* in words that have the vowel sounds split? The rule is, **"In spelling words in which the *ie/ei* vowel combination is split, use** _____ (*ie/ei*)."

ie

40

We now have a rule that applies to split sounds of *ie/ei.* Complete the following blanks: conven____nt, len____nt, propr____ty, carr____r, cour____r, and var____ty.

All are *ie.*

41

In your own words, write this rule that you discovered. "**_____."

Split vowel sound of *ie* is spelled *ie.*

(**Caution:** This rule could not apply to combinations resulting from the addition of a prefix or suffix that begins with an *i* to a word root that ends with an *e.* EXAMPLES: *plebe/ian, spontane/ity, the/ism, re/inforce, pre/ignition.* You can hear these sounds correctly!)

42

Self-test

In Column I, fill the blank with either *ie* or *ei*. Next, check your answer at the bottom of the page. Correct any mistakes in Column I. Write the correct word twice; once in Column II, once in Column III. Pronounce the word you are spelling.

Column I	Column II	Column III
1. len____nt		
2. s____sta		
3. per d____m		
4. h____rarchy		
5. d____tary		
6. var____ty		
7. ingred____nt		
8. anx____ty		
9. recip____nt		
10. notor____ty		
11. obed____nce		
12. incip____nt		
13. propr____tor		
14. conven____nce		
15. ga____ty		

1. len*ie*nt
2. s*ie*sta
3. per d*ie*m
4. h*ie*rarchy
5. d*ie*tary
6. var*ie*ty
7. ingred*ie*nt
8. anx*ie*ty
9. recip*ie*nt
10. notor*ie*ty
11. obed*ie*nce
12. incip*ie*nt
13. propr*ie*tor
14. conven*ie*nce
15. ga*ie*ty

43

There is only one more rule about *ei* and *ie*: **"All other sounds of** *ei/ie* ***are spelled*** ei." There are only four exceptions to this rule if you exclude all three-letter words from it. (EXAMPLE: *pie*).

44

Listen to the words *forfeit, heir, weigh, eight, sleight, height, foreign,* and *vein*. How many different sounds of *ei* did you hear? _____

three
(weigh, eight, vein) *a*
(height, sleight) *i*
(foreign, forfeit, heir)

45

All sounds of *ie* or *ei* (exceptions excluded) that do not involve the long sound of *e*, the sounds of *sh* or *ch*, or the split sound of *ie/ei* are spelled with

46
Self-test

In Column I, fill the blank with either *ie* or *ei*. Next, check your answers at the bottom of the page. Correct any mistakes in Column I. Write the correct word twice; once in Column II, once in Column III. You must pronounce the word. It will need an ei/ie to complete it.

Column I	Column II	Column III
1. th____r		
2. r____gn		
3. sl____gh		
4. ____ght		
5. ____ghty		
6. fr____ght		
7. for____gn		
8. counterf____t		
9. rev____lle		
10. forf____t		
11. n____ghbor		
12. b____ge		
13. sk____n		
14. v____l		
15. w____ght		
16. h____ght		
17. h____r		
18. h____ress		
19. v____n		
20. f____gn		
21. w____gh		
22. w____ghty		
23. inv____gh		
24. inv____gle		
25. h____nous		

If you missed any word, you should check the rules to learn why you missed it. Chances are it was because you heard the sound incorrectly!

1. the*i*r	9. rev*ei*lle	17. h*ei*r
2. r*ei*gn	10. forf*ei*t	18. h*ei*ress
3. sl*ei*gh	11. n*ei*ghbor	19. v*ei*n
4. *ei*ght	12. b*ei*ge	20. f*ei*gn
5. *ei*ghty	13. sk*ei*n	21. w*ei*gh
6. fr*ei*ght	14. v*ei*l	22. w*ei*ghty
7. for*ei*gn	15. w*ei*ght	23. inv*ei*gh
8. counterf*ei*t	16. h*ei*ght	24. inv*ei*gle
		25. h*ei*nous

47

Now for the words that are exceptions to your last rule for spelling words with *ei* or *ie* in them. Here is a nonsense rhyme. (Exceptions and words to connect them with are italicized.)

The girl with the s*ie*ve sifting sand by the sea
Is making a sand p*ie* for a fr*ie*nd and for me.
Her fr*ie*nd, the l*ie*utenant, was heard to mutter,
    then cry,
"In l*ie*u of a p*ie* I shall l*ie* down and d*ie*."
Now t*ie* this together, explain it to me;
Must I eat a sand p*ie* while watching the sea?

List the four words that are exceptions to the rule that all other sounds of *ie/ei* use *ei*.

1. _____ *Check answer;*   sieve
2. _____ *then write*   friend
3. _____ *7 times.*   lieutenant
4. _____   lieu

_____   _____

_____   _____

_____   _____

_____   _____

_____   _____

_____   _____

_____   _____

_____   _____

_____   _____

_____   _____

48

Can you write a rhyme of your own? Use any device that will help you remember fr__nd, s__ve, l__utenant, and l__u.

All are *ie*.

49

In the following exception-learning device:

> There was a young sh*ei*k, an Iraqi,
> Who was a wild, w*ei*rd, hep disc jockey.
> With n*ei*ther sleep nor l*ei*sure
> He suffered a s*ei*zure,
> Which *ei*ther meant rest or be rocky.

The italicized words are exceptions to the rule,
"** _____

_____."

i before *e* except after *c* when the sound of *e* is long.

50

In the following exception-learning device:

> A *financier* is a good friend to have.

The italicized word is an exception to the rule,
"** _____

_____."

i before *e* except after *c* when the sound of *e* is long.

51

In the following exception-learning device:

> The girl with the s*ie*ve sifting sand by the
>   sea
> Is making a sand *pie* for a *friend* and for
>   me.
> Her *friend,* the *lieutenant,* was heard to
>   mutter, then cry,
> "In *lieu* of a *pie* I shall *lie* down and *die.*"
> Now *tie* this together, explain it to me;
> Must I eat a sand *pie* while watching the
>   sea?

The italicized words are exceptions to the rule,
"** _____

_____."

All sounds of *ie/ei* that do not involve the long sound of *e, sh, ch,* or split sound are spelled with *ei.*

52

Now summarize four rules for spelling words that have the vowel combination *ie/ei* in them. If necessary, you may look back.

Rule 1.

With the long sound of *e,* use **_____
_____.

Exceptions to the rule are: _____,
_____,   _____,
_____,   _____,
_____   _____.

(Remember the limerick and who is a good friend to have.)

> *i* before *e* except after *c*
>
> sheik, weird, neither, either, leisure, seize (seizure), financier

53
Rule 2.

When there is a *sh* or *ch* sound before the vowel combination, use _____ (*ei/ie*).

> *ie*

54
Rule 3.

When there is a split vowel sound involving the vowels *ie* or *ei,* use _____.

> *ie*

55
Rule 4.

All other sounds of *ei/ie* use _____, except in the words _____, _____, _____, and _____.

> *ei*
> sieve, friend, lieutenant, lieu

56

If you had these last four frames completely correct, you are remarkable! If you missed any, review what you missed and learn them better.

57
Self-test

Work this self-test as you have the others. Pronounce aloud the word you are spelling. Remember all blanks will require *ie* or *ei*. Correct answers are at the bottom of the page.

Column I	Column II	Column III
1. br____f	_____	_____
2. p____ce	_____	_____
3. conc____ve	_____	_____
4. pat____nt	_____	_____
5. ga____ty	_____	_____
6. w____rd	_____	_____
7. d____t	_____	_____
8. v____l	_____	_____
9. s____ve	_____	_____
10. financ____r	_____	_____
11. rec____ve	_____	_____
12. notor____ty	_____	_____
13. ach____ve	_____	_____
14. s____ze	_____	_____
15. conc____t	_____	_____
16. w____gh	_____	_____
17. counterf____t	_____	_____
18. l____utenant	_____	_____
19. y____ld	_____	_____
20. ser____s	_____	_____
21. c____lings	_____	_____
22. sh____ld	_____	_____
23. n____ghbor	_____	_____
24. br____r	_____	_____
25. for____gn	_____	_____

Any word missed should be checked with the rules to understand why it was missed. Chances are it was because the sound was heard incorrectly!

1. brief	9. sieve	17. counterfeit
2. piece	10. financier	18. lieutenant
3. conceive	11. receive	19. yield
4. patient	12. notoriety	20. series
5. gaiety	13. achieve	21. ceilings
6. weird	14. seize	22. shield
7. diet	15. conceit	23. neighbor
8. veil	16. weigh	24. brier
		25. foreign

4 final *y* to *i*

1

You may think we have made a fuss about hearing sounds correctly. We haven't. Even though the examples you have had with the *ie/ei* rules are simple sounds, you still have to ** _____ them correctly.

hear *or* pronounce and hear

2

If you learn to hear simple sounds correctly, soon you will learn to hear more complicated words _____ (how).

correctly

3

Learning spelling rules will improve your spelling ability. However, if you do not hear correctly the word to which the rule applies, you could still spell it ** _____ (how).

incorrectly, wrong

4

You know the *ie/ei* rule for the word *misch____f.* How about its adjectival form? Is it pronounced *mis′ chi vous* or *mis che′ vi ous?* If you do not know the correct pronunciation, look in the dictionary. See how the correct pronunciation keeps you from making a mistake in spelling. The correct spelling of this adjective from *misch____f* is _____.

ie

ie
mischievous

5

You know how to apply the *ie/ei* rules to *l____uten-ant.* Spell *loo ten′ an cy.* Be sure to say it aloud and listen first. It is spelled _____.

ie

lieutenancy

6

Frames 4 and 5 have given you a hint about how important it is to say a word correctly and ** _____ what you say.

hear *or* listen to

7

If you pronounce words well, you will probably learn to spell rapidly. If you do not pronounce words well, use a dictionary for pronunciation whenever you are unsure. It will take you a little longer to learn to spell correctly, but you will be learning two things at once. Everyone should be able to spell **_____.

correctly

8

A game you can play as you learn to pronounce and hear correctly is to listen to the way many people mispronounce words. Of course, you won't correct them! You *will* feel good about your achievement. Even listen to people on radio and television. When you *hear* them say a word wrong, remember they have a secretary to spell it for them. This is a game that increases in fun as you say and hear more **_____ (how).

correctly

9

The next rule to learn is a simple one. It tells you when to change a *y* on the end of a word to *i* before adding other endings.

10

Final *y* preceded by a CONSONANT becomes *i* before all endings except those endings beginning with *i*.

 beauty + ful becomes beautiful
 easy + ly becomes _____

easily

11

Final *y* preceded by a consonant becomes *i* before all endings except endings beginning with *i*.

 pity + ful becomes _____
 pity + ed becomes _____
  but
 pity + ing becomes_____

pitiful
pitied

pitying

12

You can't beat this *saying, hearing,* and *thinking* combination.

marry + age becomes _____   marriage
marry + ed   becomes _____   married
marry + ing becomes _____   marrying

13

fly + er   becomes _____   flier
fly + ing becomes _____   flying
fly + es   becomes _____   flies

14

Are you solving some old problems?

ready + er   becomes _____   readier
ready + est becomes _____   readiest
ready + ly   becomes _____   readily
ready + ing becomes _____   readying

15

gratify + cation becomes _____   gratification
history + cal   becomes _____   historical
amplify + ing   becomes _____   amplifying
tragedy + es   becomes _____   tragedies

16

biology + cal becomes _____   biological
ninety   + es becomes _____   nineties
ninety   + eth becomes _____   ninetieth

17

When you take lonely + ness to form _____
_____, you are using the rule, "Final *y* pre-   loneliness
ceded by a consonant becomes **_____
_____."   *i* before all endings ex-
                                                               cept those beginning
                                                               with *i*

18

When you take copy + ing to form _____,   copying
you are using the rule, "Final *y* preceded by **___   a consonant becomes
_____."   *i* before all endings ex-
                                                               cept those beginning
                                                               with *i.*

19

When you take heavy + est to form _____,
you are using the rule, "** _____
_____."

heaviest

Final y preceded by a consonant becomes *i* before all endings except those endings beginning with *i*.

This is a story to form a picture.

This picture should help you remember five* exceptions to the rule you have just learned about final *y*.

Once upon a time, a long time ago—a time when gallant knights courted fair ladies—

beauty was spelled beaute
bounty was spelled bounte
duty was spelled dute
plenty was spelled plente
pity was spelled pite

To help remember the time and these words, form a mental picture of a very gallant knight on a white horse. He is sitting on his horse at the bottom of a tower. At a window, high in the tower, is an exceedingly beautiful damsel. She is dressed in a flowing white gown and wears a high, pointed, white hat with a white flowing scarf attached. Form the picture here.

* It is possible that there are more than these five words that have kept the Middle English spelling. You are not too likely to meet them, though, for they have not shown up after careful search of several sources.

Now hear the knight singing to the lady in the
tower—

> My beloved so beauteous,
> My love's more than duteous—
> It's endlessly bounteous!
> My state will be piteous
> If your love isn't plenteous,
> Beloved so beauteous, be mine!

You can learn eous words by learning the little rhymes on the last page.

or try

Beauty is praised;
Bounty is blessed;
Duty endured;
Pity expressed.
Plenty—a dream of the world.

or a system using

B
B
D
P
P

for example:

B bad
B boys
D don't
P please
P parents

You may even want to write the eous exceptions. The system that helps you learn them best is fine.

Use this information only if you need it.

Vowels are *a, e, i, o, u,* and sometimes *w* and *y.*

Say and listen to:

a–lay	*a*pple	*a*ny
e–enough	b*e*t	b*e*g
i–ice	*i*n	*i*t
o–over	*o*f	*o*ff
u–d*u*ty	*u*nder	*u*p

W and *y* are vowels when they have a vowel sound.

Say and listen to:

Vowel Sound	*Consonant Sound*
de*w*	de*w*y
sho*w*	sho*w*y
pa*w*	*w*hip
pa*y*	*w*ear
pra*y*	*y*ou
to*y*	*y*oung

20

There is only one other situation in which final *y* can occur. That occurs when the *y* is preceded by a vowel. When final *y* is preceded by a _____, keep the *y* before all endings. (There are exceptions to this rule, but they are so easy they are not worth bothering with.)

vowel

Only for the very curious:

lay–laid *but* layer, laying, layman
pay–paid *but* payer, paying, payment
say–said *but* saying, says
day–daily *but* daylight, daytime
gay–gaily, gaiety *but* gayness, gaysome

21

When the final *y* is preceded by a vowel, keep the *y*.

buy	+ er	becomes _____	buyer
buy	+ ing	becomes _____	buying
enjoy	+ able	becomes _____	enjoyable
enjoy	+ ing	becomes _____	enjoying

22

employ	+ er	becomes _____	employer
employ	+ ment	becomes _____	employment
employ	+ able	becomes _____	employable
employ	+ ing	becomes _____	employing

23

convey	+ ance	becomes _____	conveyance
portray	+ al	becomes _____	portrayal
survey	+ or	becomes _____	surveyor
deploy	+ ment	becomes _____	deployment

24

When you take *buy + ing* to form _____, you are using the rule, "When final *y* is preceded by a vowel, ** _____."

buying

keep the *y*

25

When you take *convoy + ed* to form _____, you are using the rule, "When final *y* is preceded by a ** _____."

convoyed

vowel, keep the *y*

26

When you take *enjoy + able* to form _____, you are using the rule, "** _____."

enjoyable

When final *y* is preceded by a vowel, keep the *y* before all endings.

27
Self-test

In Column II, write the correct word. Next, check your answers at the bottom of the page. Correct any mistakes in Column II. Write your correct answer in Column III.

Column I	Column II	Column III
1. identify + cation	_____	_____
2. victory + ous	_____	_____
3. convoy + ed	_____	_____
4. liquefy + er	_____	_____
5. pedagogy + cal	_____	_____
6. wealthy + est	_____	_____
7. remedy + al	_____	_____
8. delay + ed	_____	_____
9. delay + ing	_____	_____
10. copy + ing	_____	_____
11. pity + ful	_____	_____
12. enjoy + able	_____	_____
13. employ + ment	_____	_____
14. beauty + ful	_____	_____
15. survey + or	_____	_____

1. identification	6. wealthiest	11. pitiful
2. victorious	7. remedial	12. enjoyable
3. convoyed	8. delayed	13. employment
4. liquefier	9. delaying	14. beautiful
5. pedagogical	10. copying	15. surveyor

28

From the following two lists of words, figure out two exceptions that keep the *y*.

ladylike	ladyship
citylike	secretaryship
countrylike	suretyship

**_____.

Keep the *y* when adding *like* or *ship*.

29

Study the derivatives of *one-syllable adjectives* and find another exception to the "keep the final *y*" rule.

dry	drier	dryly	dryness
shy	shier	shyly	shyness
sly	slier	slyly	slyness

When spelling words built from one-syllable adjectives, **_____.

Keep the *y* before *ly* and *ness*.

30

The exceptions in frames 28 and 29 are so easy that you probably spell them correctly anyhow. They were put in to make the record complete. If for any reason you feel you need to learn them, practice building your own *like, ship, ly,* and *ness* words and check with the dictionary.

31

Does meaning or sound or do both affect:

　　business and busyness?

(*Dictionary if necessary!*)

You can hear the difference! Also different meaning.

USE WHAT YOU HAVE LEARNED

What you have learned is only yours so long as you use it. Even if you are not confident about this rule, USE IT. *Then* look up the word in the dictionary.

5   spelling noun plurals

1

In Chapter 1, you were given a reference page that told you when to double a final consonant. In this chapter, try to prepare a reference page of your own as you work through the chapter.

You can start with the first rule.

2

The first rule for spelling noun plurals is that **you usually add** *s* **to the singular.** The plural of *book* is *books*. The plural of *car* is _____.

cars

3

The plural of *dog* is *dogs*.
The plural of *cat* is _____.
The plural of *rat* is _____.

cats
rats

4

The plural of *apartment* is *apartments*.
The plural of *bushel*   is _____.
The plural of *sister*   is _____.
The plural of *feature*   is _____.

bushels
sisters
features

5

The plural of *value*   is _____.
The plural of *cashier* is _____.
The plural of *skill*   is _____.
The plural of *taxi*   is _____.
The plural of *alibi*   is _____.

values
cashiers
skills
taxis
alibis

6

The second rule for spelling noun plurals is, **"With common or proper nouns ending in the sound of** *s (ss, x, sh, ch, z)* **add** *es.*" The plural of *bush* is *bushes*. The plural of *loss* is _____.

losses

7

The plural of *watch*　　is *watches.*
The plural of *chorus*　is ＿＿＿＿＿＿.　choruses
The plural of *dress*　　is ＿＿＿＿＿＿.　dresses
The plural of *dispatch* is ＿＿＿＿＿＿.　dispatches

8

The plural of *Otis*　　is *Otises.*
The plural of *sash*　　is ＿＿＿＿＿＿.　sashes
The plural of *annex*　is ＿＿＿＿＿＿.　annexes
The plural of *climax* is ＿＿＿＿＿＿.　climaxes

9

The plural of *Lois*　　is ＿＿＿＿＿＿.　Loises
The plural of *tax*　　　is ＿＿＿＿＿＿.　taxes
The plural of *mattress* is ＿＿＿＿＿＿.　mattresses
The plural of *Hirsh*　is ＿＿＿＿＿＿.　Hirshes
The plural of *church*　is ＿＿＿＿＿＿.　churches

10

The plural of *Phillips* is ＿＿＿＿＿＿.　Phillipses
The plural of *suffix*　is ＿＿＿＿＿＿.　suffixes
The plural of *witch*　is ＿＿＿＿＿＿.　witches
The plural of *bass*　　is ＿＿＿＿＿＿.　basses
The plural of *Katz*　　is ＿＿＿＿＿＿.　Katzes

11

The plural of *count*　is ＿＿＿＿＿＿.　counts
The plural of *bonus*　is ＿＿＿＿＿＿.　bonuses
The plural of *parish*　is ＿＿＿＿＿＿.　parishes
The plural of *expense* is ＿＿＿＿＿＿.　expenses
The plural of *record*　is ＿＿＿＿＿＿.　records

Are you preparing your reference page?

12

The third rule for spelling plurals deals with numbers and letters. Add *'s*. The plural of the letter *A* is *A*'s. The plural of the letter *B* is ＿＿＿＿＿＿.　B's

13

The plural of *X* is *X*'s.
The plural of *C* is _____.   C's
The plural of *1* is _____.   1's
The plural of *2* is _____.   2's

14

The plural of *Z* is _____.   Z's
The plural of *4* is _____.   4's
The plural of *6* is _____.   6's
The plural of *D* is _____.   D's
The plural of *M* is _____.   M's

15

The next rule for forming noun plurals deals with
nouns ending in *y*. There are three easy parts to
this rule.   *Two parts should
                                                 sound familiar.*

16

**With nouns ending in *y* preceded by a vowel,
add *s*.** The plural of *day* is *days*. The plural of *key*
is _____.   keys

17

The plural of *attorney* is *attorneys*.
The plural of *journey* is _____.   journeys
The plural of *convoy* is _____.   convoys
The plural of *Friday* is _____.   Fridays

18

The plural of *corduroy* is _____.   corduroys
The plural of *holiday* is _____.   holidays
The plural of *alloy* is _____.   alloys
The plural of *Monday* is _____.   Mondays
The plural of *turkey* is _____.   turkeys

19

**With nouns ending in *y* preceded by a con-
sonant, change the *y* to *i* and add *es*.** The plural
of *cruelty* is *cruelties*. The plural of *enemy* is
_____.   enemies

20

The plural of *company* is *companies.*
The plural of *seventy* is _____.   seventies
The plural of *property* is _____.   properties
The plural of *security* is _____.   securities

21

The plural of *notary*   is _____.   notaries
The plural of *valley*   is _____.   valleys
The plural of *society* is _____.   societies
The plural of *burglary* is _____.   burglaries

22

The plural of *railway* is _____.   railways
The plural of *theory* is _____.   theories
The plural of *vacancy* is _____.   vacancies
The plural of *alley*   is _____.   alleys

23

**With all *proper* nouns ending in *y*, the plural is
formed by adding *s*.** The plural of *Mary* is
Marys. The plural of *Stanley* is _____.   Stanleys

24

The plural of *Kelly*   is *Kellys.*
The plural of *Harry*   is _____.   Harrys
The plural of *Ruby*   is _____.   Rubys
The plural of *O'Malley* is _____.   O'Malleys

25

The plural of *Lucy* is _____.   Lucys
The plural of *Rhey* is _____.   Rheys
The plural of *Kay*   is _____.   Kays
The plural of *Kenny* is _____.   Kennys
The plural of *Leroy* is _____.   Leroys

26

The plural of *forgery* is _____.   forgeries
The plural of *chimney* is _____.   chimneys
The plural of *money*   is _____.   moneys
The plural of *Sally*   is _____.   Sallys
The plural of *quantity* is _____.   quantities

27

The plural of *yesterday* is _____.		yesterdays
The plural of *currency* is _____.		currencies
The plural of *Harry* is _____.		Harrys
The plural of *novelty* is _____.		novelties

28

The plural of *trophy* is _____.		trophies
The plural of *Levey* is _____.		Leveys
The plural of *Saturday* is _____.		Saturdays
The plural of *warranty* is _____.		warranties

On the reference page that you are preparing, do you have four rules, one of which has three parts? If so, you are correct. If not, check and correct.

29
Self-test

In Column II, write the correct form of the plural for the word in Column I. Next, check your answers at the bottom of the page. Correct any mistakes in Column II. Write your correct answer in Column III.

Column I	Column II	Column III
1. brother	_____	_____
2. mile	_____	_____
3. monkey	_____	_____
4. address	_____	_____
5. breach	_____	_____
6. summary	_____	_____
7. McNalley	_____	_____
8. 6	_____	_____
9. Pentz	_____	_____
10. Smith	_____	_____
11. service	_____	_____
12. Thomas	_____	_____
13. entry	_____	_____
14. eighty	_____	_____
15. climax	_____	_____

1. brothers	6. summaries	11. services
2. miles	7. McNalleys	12. Thomases
3. monkeys	8. 6's	13. entries
4. addresses	9. Pentzes	14. eighties
5. breaches	10. Smiths	15. climaxes

30

There are other rules about the formation of plurals. Some nouns change form entirely when they become plural. Hear the difference in sound between *foot* and *feet*.

31

Hear the difference in sound between:

Singular	Plural
mouse	mice
man	men
goose	geese
tooth	teeth
child	children

32

Some words ending in *f sounds* change form also. You can learn to hear this difference, too. Listen to the singular *half* and its plural *halves*.

33

Listen to:

Singular	Plural
self	selves
thief	thieves
shelf	shelves
but	
belief	beliefs

34

Listen to:

Singular	Plural
elf	elves
half	halves
life	lives
but	
rebuff	rebuffs

35

Try to spell the plural of:

Singular	Plural
ourself	_____
tariff	_____
leaf	_____
wife	_____

ourselves
tariffs
leaves
wives

36

Another group of words in which you can hear the plural is compound nouns. **The rule for compound nouns is to make the most important part of the word (usually the noun) plural.** Study and listen to:

Singular	Plural
lieutenant colonel	lieutenant colonels
brother-in-law	brothers-in-law

Did you hear it?
Did you determine the noun?

37

Study and listen to:

Singular	Plural
notary public	notaries public
master sergeant	master sergeants
court-martial	courts-martial
commander-in-chief	commanders-in-chief

Did you hear it?
Is the noun made plural?

38

There is no need to develop frames 36 and 37 because you are learning to spell by sound. The reason for not developing this thought is that you can **_____ the plural.

hear or detect

39

If you feel that your grammar is weak in the compound-word department, you can correct it with any good textbook of English grammar. This is a course in spelling by sound plus some rules and principles. The spelling of compound nouns will be based on your **_____ them.

hearing or listening to

40

This brings you to the last rule for forming plurals when the sounds are the same: **Nouns that end in o are** *usually* **made plural by adding** *s*. The plural of *desperado* is *desperados*. The plural of *bolero* is _____.

boleros

41

The plural of *Eskimo* is *Eskimos*.
The plural of *magneto* is _____.
The plural of *tòbacco* is _____.
The plural of *inferno* is _____.

magnetos
tobaccos
infernos

42

The plural of *mikado* is _____.
The plural of *torso* is _____.
The plural of *burro* is _____.
The plural of *bronco* is _____.

mikados
torsos
burros
broncos

43

Musical terms that end in *o* follow the rule of adding *s*. The plural of *piano* is formed by adding _____ to the singular.

s

44

The plural of *soprano* is *sopranos*.
The plural of *alto* is _____.
The plural of *contralto* is _____.
The plural of *concerto* is _____.

altos
contraltos
concertos

45

The plural of *piccolo* is _____.
The plural of *trio* is _____.
The plural of *crescendo* is _____.
The plural of *adagio* is _____.

piccolos
trios
crescendos
adagios

46

If you are forming the plural of a noun that ends in *o* and is related to music, you are safe in using the rule, "Nouns ending in *o* are made plural by adding _____."

s

47

When you take the musical direction *fortissimo* and form its plural, _____, you are using the rule, "** _____ _____."

fortissimos

Musically related nouns ending in *o* are pluralized by adding *s*.

48

When you form the plural of *dynamo,* which is _____, you are using the rule, "** _____ _____."

dynamos
Nouns ending in *o* are usually made plural by adding *s*.

49

You are also safe in using *s* when forming plurals of nouns ending in *o* if the *o* is preceded by a vowel (*a, e, i, o, u,* and in this rule *w* and *y* also). The plural of *patio* is *patios*. The plural of *folio* is _____.

folios

50

The plural of *pistachio* is *pistachios*.
The plural of *studio* is _____.
The plural of *shampoo* is _____.
The plural of *curio* is _____.
The plural of *igloo* is _____.

studios
shampoos
curios
igloos

51

The plural of *rodeo* is _____.
The plural of *solo* is _____.
The plural of *scenario* is _____.
The plural of *flamingo* is _____.
The plural of *cuckoo* is _____.

rodeos
solos
scenarios
flamingos
cuckoos

52

Are you listening and asking, "Which part of the rule?" You should be. Exceptions are coming up soon.

The plural of *silo*   is _____.

The plural of *embryo* is _____.

The plural of *portfolio* is _____.

The plural of *oratorio* is _____.

The plural of *banjo*   is _____.

silos
embryos
portfolios
oratorios
banjos

53

The plural of *vibrato* is _____.

The plural of *ratio*   is _____.

The plural of *ego*   is _____.

The plural of *cello*   is _____.

vibratos
ratios
egos
cellos

54

Nouns that end in *o* usually are made plural by adding ____.

s

55

When you pluralize memento, you are using the rule, "**_____.**"

Nouns ending in *o* are usually made plural by adding *s*.

56

Two special groups of words to which the rule in frame 54 applies are **_____ and **_____.

musical words and words with final *o* preceded by a vowel

57

The rule in frame 54 and its accent in frame 55 have been developed quite extensively because there are many exceptions to the base rule (frame 54). Study the next page carefully.

The following words are customarily made plural by adding es.

The number of these words that you need to know in order for the rule to be effective can only be determined by you or your teacher. What you learn from this list is up to you. Learn the words you are likely to use. Use any method you care to devise.

If you use Webster's Third New International Dictionary, and you are certain that the person evaluating your spelling is aware of the changes it allows, you can reduce this list by 15 words. These recently permitted spellings are indicated by the second parentheses (s).

archipelago (es) (s)
buffalo (es)
domino (es) (s)
echo (es)
embargo (es)
fresco (es) (s)
ginkgo (es)
hero (es)
hobo (es) (s)
innuendo (es) (s)
mango (es) (s)
magnifico (es) (s)
manifesto (es) (s)
mosquito (es) (s)
motto (es) (s)
mulatto (es) (s)
Negro (es)
peccadillo (es) (s)
portico (es) (s)
potato (es)
tomato (es)
tornado (es) (s)
torpedo (es)
veto (es)
volcano (es) (s)

58

By now, you should have finished your reference page.

Does your reference page look something like this?

Formation of Noun Plurals

1. Most nouns are made plural by adding *s*.

2. Common and proper nouns ending in the sound of *s* are pluralized by adding *es*.

3. Letters and numbers are pluralized by adding *'s*.

4. Nouns ending in *y:*
   a. If *y* is preceded by a vowel, add *s*.
   b. If *y* is preceded by a consonant, change *y* to *i* and add *es*.
   c. All proper nouns ending in *y* are made plural by adding *s*.

5. Some nouns are pluralized by changing form. Listen for the sound and spell the plural as it sounds.

6. Nouns ending in *o* are *usually* made plural by adding *s*.
   a. True with musical words.
   b. True if *o* is preceded by a vowel.
   c. List of 25 exceptions to be learned as *needed*.

Information for Chapter 6

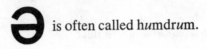

is often called h*u*mdr*u*m.

has a sound that can be repre-
sented by any of the vowels.

ə is the sound of
a in *a*go
e in ag*e*nt
i in san*i*ty
o in c*o*mply
u in foc*u*s

In fact, ə is the vowel sound heard in

h*u*mdr*u*m

This chapter is fairly difficult but MOST valuable.
Work SLOWLY and thoughtfully through it, and it
will repay you well!

6   which vowel?

1

A big stumbling block in spelling is how to tell which vowel to use in the word root when the syllable is NOT accented. In the word *syllable,* do you hear a distinct *a* sound? _____ (yes/no).

no

2

Syllable is pronounced *sil′ ə b'l.* The sign ə could represent *a, e, i, o,* or *u.* Which vowel is it? Find the same word root in another word—one that accents the questionable vowel. Say *syllabic (syl lab′ ic).* The vowel sound you can now hear is clearly an ___ (*a/e/i/o/u*).

a

3

When you hear the *a* in *syl lab′ ic,* you know how to spell *syll___ble.*

a

4

Listen as you pronounce *compilation (com pə la′ shən).* There is no distinct *i* sound in the second syllable. Which vowel does the ə sound represent? Try the word *compile (com pīl′).* When you hear the *i* in compile, you know how to spell *comp___lation.*

i

5

In your dictionary, find the word *correlate (kor′ ə lat),* or *correlation (kor ə la′ shən).* Read the part in brackets [   ]. What word do you find as a key word for the vowel in the second syllable of *correlate* or *correlation?* _____

relate

6

In your dictionary, read the definition of the word *dilatation (dil ə ta′ tion).* In the meaning given, can you find a key word to give the sound of *a* for the second syllable of *dilatation?* It is _____.

dilation

7

In your dictionary, find the word *scholar* (*skŏl′ ər*).
Can you find a word beginning with the word root
schol that will give you the sound of *a* in *scholar?*
It is _____.

scholastic
(skə las′ tik)

8

Without using your dictionary, try to think of a
word that will serve as a key for the italicized
vowel in the following words:

narr*a*tive (*nar′ ə tiv*) _____

relative (*rel′ ə tiv*) _____

narrate (narration)
relate (relation)

9

In the following words, the vowel with the ə sound
is omitted. Pronounce the word. Think of a key
word. Write the key word and then place the correct vowel in its blank space.

Which Vowel   *Key Word*

a. comp___tition   _____

b. conf___dent   _____

c. res___dent   _____

e—compete
i—confide
i—reside

10

By thinking or using your dictionary, complete the
following. (Be careful to use the same word root in
your key word.)

a. coll___ge   _____

b. aut___mn   _____

c. mir___cle   _____

d. monot___nous   _____

e. amb___guity   _____

e—collegiate
u—autumnal
a—miraculous
o—monotone or tone
i—ambiguous

11

The following words come from the Latin root
meaning "time."

temp ə rary
temp ə ral
extemp ə raneous
contemp ə rary

From this same root, find in your dictionary a short
key word, *temp___*.

temp*o*

12

Using the key word, *tempo*:

temporary	becomes	_____	temporary
temporal	becomes	_____	temporal
extemporaneous	becomes	_____	extemporaneous
contemporary	becomes	_____	contemporary

13

From the Latin root, *memor,* meaning "remember," come the words:

> mem′ ə ra bil′ ia
> mem′ ə rable
> mem′ ə ran′ dum
> mem′ ə ry

Find a key word with the accent on the second syllable. It is _____.

memor′ial

memərabilia	becomes	_____	memorabilia
memərable	becomes	_____	memorable
memərandum	becomes	_____	memorandum
meməry	becomes	_____	memory

14

The Latin root, *metr,* means measure. Notice the following:

> thermom ə ter
> speedom ə ter
> m ə trical

Can you think of (or find) a key word that lets you hear the *e* in *metr* words? It is _____.

meter

thermoməter	becomes	_____	thermometer
speedoməter	becomes	_____	speedometer
mətrical	becomes	_____	metrical

15

The Latin word for body is *corpus.* Pronounce the following:

> corp′ ə rate
> corp′ ə ration
> corp′ ə rator

Look up *corpər* words in your dictionary and find a key word that makes the ə sound clear. The key word is _____.

corpor′eal

corpərate	becomes	_____	corporate
corpəration	becomes	_____	corporation
corpərator	becomes	_____	corporator

16
Self-test

Following is a list of words and a blank for a key word in which you can hear the vowel that is a ə-sound in the first word. Try to think of a key word from the *same root*. If you cannot think of one, find one in your dictionary. First write the key word in its blank. Then insert the correct missing vowel in Column I. After you have finished, check your answers at the bottom of the page.

Column I	Key Word
1. res____gnation	_____
2. m____terial	_____
3. conserv____tive	_____
4. democr____**cy**	_____
5. comp____tent	_____
6. appl____cation	_____
7. or____gin	_____
8. sim____lar	_____
9. const____tution	_____
10. merc____ry	_____
11. hypocr____sy	_____
12. med____cine	_____
13. ecst____sy	_____
14. adm____ration	_____
15. symp____thy	_____

After you have gone to the trouble to find a key word, try to remember it so you won't have to look it up again. Usually just writing it and its meaning will fix it in your mind. Frequently looking at its origin (in the brackets [   ] following the word) is enough to make you remember it.

You may have found or thought of different key words. If so, check their pronunciation in your dictionary. If your word agrees with the dictionary, use it. What is natural for YOU will be easier to remember.

1.	i	resign	6.	i	appliance	11.	i	hypocrite
2.	a	matter	7.	i	original	12.	i	medicinal
3.	a	conservation	8.	i	similitude	13.	a	ecstatic
4.	a	democratic	9.	i	constituent	14.	i	admire
		(democrat)	10.	u	mercurial	15.	a	pathos
5.	e	compete						

Same principle used with CAUTION. Work SLOWLY through the next section. *Think!*

17

This principle of shifting the ə sound to an accented syllable can be used with two groups of problem suffixes. For one group of problem suffixes, examine the following two lists:

arbitrAry	cemetEry
centenAry	confectionEry
commentAry	drudgEry
contemporAry	forgEry
disciplinAry	hatchEry
documentAry	monastEry
elementAry	mystEry
fragmentAry	recovEry
infirmAry	savagEry
librAry	treachEry

18

Pronounce some of the *ary/ery* words. Listen to what you say. When pronounced, do *ary/ery* sound alike? _____(yes/no)

yes

19

Using the first word on the list in frame 17, ask yourself, "Can *arbitr* connect with *a* in an accented form?" You will probably think of a key word, *arbitrAtion* (or *arbitrAte*), almost immediately. (You can use your dictionary if necessary.) Thinking of arbitrAtion, you can spell arbitr____ry.

a

20

Using the first word on the *ery* list ask yourself, "Can *cemet* connect with *a* in an accented form?" _____ (yes/no)

no

21

Ask yourself the "a" question using the word root *annivers*. Could you find a key word for anniversary? _____ (yes/no)

no

22

Study what you have learned in frames 19, 20, and 21. Draw a conclusion. The accent-shift "a" principle will save time and errors ONLY **_____
_____.

Read frame 23 for the entire answer.

23

1. when the word to be spelled ends with the sound of *ary/ery* and

2. when the word root connects with *a* in an accented form (*ate, ation, ator*).

When these two conditions apply, use _____.

ary

Continue working CAUTIOUSLY
　　　　　　　　SLOWLY
　　　　　　　　THOUGHTFULLY.

24

While thinking of the word *anniver***sary**, draw another conclusion. The accent-shift "a" principle does NOT help with *all* words that end in the sound *ary/ery* and are spelled _____.

ary

25

You may think this a serious limitation for help in using *ary/ery*. It is the best that can be done. It will be a big saver in time and errors as you learn key words and remember them.

26
Self-test

Find key words for the accent-shift "a" principle for the following *ary* words. Check your key words at the bottom of the page. If your key words use the same word root and you prefer them, use them. They may be easier to remember.

1. centenary _____
2. commentary _____
3. contemporary _____
4. disciplinary _____
5. documentary _____
6. elementary _____
7. fragmentary _____
8. infirmary _____
9. library _____
10. itinerary _____
11. insanitary _____
12. luminary _____
13. military _____
14. ordinary _____
15. preliminary _____
16. rotary _____
17. sanitary _____
18. notary _____
19. summary _____
20. temporary _____

If you keep this list growing in your own mind as you solve *ary*/*ery* problems, you will soon find yourself using the dictionary only rarely for this problem.

1. centenarian
2. commentator
3. contemporaneous
   (*or* temporality)
4. disciplinarian
5. documentation
6. elementarily
7. fragmentation
8. af*firm*ation
9. librarian
10. itinerate
    (*or* itineration)
11. sanitation
12. illumination
13. militate
14. ordinate
    (*or* ordination)
15. elimination
    (*or* eliminate)
16. rotation
17. sanitation
18. notate
19. summation
20. temporality (*or* contemporaneous)

stationAry
stationEry

Pronounced the same. Which is which?

An
Envelope
is
stationEry (writing materials—
         paper and Envelopes).

BONUS—used for correspondEnce!

A
stAtue
cannot move—
is
stationAry.

27
For the other group of problem suffixes, examine
the following two lists:

authoriZe	advertiSe
commercialiZe	compriSe
demobiliZe	compromiSe
federaliZe	despiSe
generaliZe	disguiSe
immuniZe	exerciSe
legaliZe	franchiSe
memoriZe	paradiSe
nationaliZe	surmiSe
visualiZe	surpriSe

only 2 *yze* words—*analyze* and *paralyze*

"My brain is paralyzed from analyzing *ize*."

28

Pronounce *authorize* and *advertise*. Do *ise* and *ize* sound alike? _____ (yes/no)

yes

29

The accent-shift system can be used to a limited extent to help with these two endings. If you can end the word with *ization* instead of *ize/ise,* use *ize.* There is a noun *civilization.* The verb is *civil*_____.

ize

30

Form verbs ending in *ize/ise* from the same word root as the following nouns:

a.	authorization	_____	authorize
b.	cauterization	_____	cauterize
c.	decentralization	_____	decentralize *or* centralize
d.	extemporization	_____	extemporize

31

Form verbs ending in *ize/ise* from the same roots as the following nouns:

a.	fertilization	_____	fertilize
b.	generalization	_____	generalize
c.	immunization	_____	immunize
d.	legalization	_____	legalize

32

Build verbs that end in *ize/ise* from the following roots:

a.	local	_____	localize
b.	material	_____	materialize
c.	national	_____	nationalize
d.	organ	_____	organize

33

Not all *ize* words will take *ization.* There is no *journalization,* but there is a *journalize.* If a word will not take *ization,* can you automatically add *ise*? _____ (yes/no)

no

34

Here again the accent-shift principle is of limited
value. Fortunately most *ize* words will take *ization*.
However, you must use care.

There is a word *improvisation* and its verb *impro-
vise*. You will remember it if you remember we are
improvi**S**ing a **S**ystem to help **S**pell *ize/ise*.

35
Self-test

With the following, construct a word ending with *ize/ise, when you can.* Write
the correct word in Column II or leave it blank. Check your answers at the bottom
of the page and correct any errors in Column III.

Column I	Column II	Column III
1. ideal		
2. rational		
3. real		
4. advert		
5. central		
6. capital		
7. parad		
8. amort		
9. fratern		
10. notor		
11. modern		
12. util		
13. franch		
14. visual		
15. crystal		

1. idealize
2. rationalize
3. realize
4. advertise or nothing at all
5. centralize
6. capitalize
7. paradise or nothing
8. amortize
9. fraternize
10. notarize
11. modernize
12. utilize
13. franchise or nothing
14. visualize
15. crystallize

This is a spelling aid that will grow in usefulness as
you use it, and as your vocabulary grows.

7 sound-alike suffixes: ion/ian—ly/ally

1

Ion and *ian* are sound-alike suffixes. In the words *dietitian* and *definition,* ion and *ian* sound **_____.

alike, the same

2

Ion and *ian* in the words *magician* and *transmission* sound **_____.

alike

3

Since *ion/ian* sound alike, you have to know something about them if you are to spell them **_____ (how).

correctly, right

4

In this chapter, you will often be forming quite new words. Because of this, you will have to pronounce the word you are forming; and _____ it correctly.

hear

5

To spell correctly, one must always _____ sounds correctly.

hear

6

For reference and directions:

ion

suffix that means:
   an action
   a condition or state
   a process
   a result

Examples:
   separation—action
   satisfaction—state or condition
   justification—process
   remuneration—result

can usually simplify to:
   action or condition

ian

suffix that means:
   of
   belonging to
   one who does (the *word root*)
   one who belongs to (the *word root*)

Examples:
   equestrian—one who rides horses
   reptilian—belonging to the group, reptiles
   barbarian—of or belonging to or one who belongs to a barbarous group

can usually simplify to:
   one who or one of

Here is the pattern for working the frames in this section: Each sentence has a blank for a word that takes *ion/ian* in some form of the word. The *basic* word is given in parentheses following the sentence. (In the first example below, the basic word is *adopt*.) Fill in the blank. The length of the blank does not give any clue to the length of the word.

Examples:

1. The _____(adoption)_____ papers were in order. (adopt)

2. It was a matter of equal _____ of lollipops. (divide)

3. He lived in Paris but was a native _____. (Georgia)

(*Answers*: (2) division; (3) Georgian)

7

Jane was impossible when she tried
_____. (navigate)   navigation

Congress was overcome by a mass of
_____. (legislate)   legislation

Everyone in the room was aware of the
_____. (tense)   tension

Only good resulted from the _____   separation
of duties. (separate)

8

The pianist was a skilled _____.   musician
(music)

Dinosaurs belonged to the _____   reptilian
class. (reptile)

She was a member of the _____   Presbyterian
church. (presbyter)

The mayor is a skilled _____.   politician
(politics)

9

"The road to hell is paved with good
_____." (intent)   intention

The student's _____ of the sun-   description
set was good. (describe)

The _____ was studying the   historian
time of Julius Caesar. (history)

A _____ on policy was finally   decision
reached. (decide)

10

After dinner, there was entertainment by a
_____. (magic)   magician

Jack's _____ for the test was   preparation
thorough. (prepare)

Warm-blooded animals that nurse their young are
_____. (mammal)   mammalians

He made a loud _____ of inno-   profession
cence. (profess)

11

Only quick action made possible the
_____ of my reservation.
(cancel)

cancellation

In order to use the library you must have an
_____ card. (identify)

identification

To spell correctly, you must pay careful
_____ to sounds. (attend)

attention

Following a swim in cold water, I have a feeling of
_____. (exhilarate)

exhilaration

12

Her grounds for divorce were _____
of affection. (alien)

alienation

The news analyst had a keen _____
of the issues. (perceive)

perception

Menus were prepared by an outstanding
_____. (diet)

dietitian

The high spot in the social season was the president's _____. (receive)

reception

13

The lenses for the binoculars were ground by a skilled _____. (optic)

optician

Jim read rapidly and with great _____.
(comprehend)

comprehension

IBM's _____ at the accountants'
_____ was well received. (exhibit)
(convene)

exhibition
convention

14

Four-year-old Peter disregarded his mother's
_____ to be careful. (admonish)

admonition

The 220 line for my new stove was installed by
an _____. (electric)

electrician

I want a telephone _____ by my
bed. (extend)

extension

He took every tax _____ he could
find. (exempt)

exemption

15

We call a medical doctor a _____. (physic)

physician

The gift of a new red rattle resulted in the baby's complete _____. (fascinate)

fascination

I learned that my account was overdrawn when the bank sent me a formal _____. (notify)

notification

Harry got the scholarship through the process of _____. (eliminate)

elimination

16
Self-test

In Column II, build a word that takes *ian* or *ion* from the word or word root of the word listed. Check your answers at the bottom of the page. Correct any errors. Write all words correctly in Column III.

Column I	Column II	Column III
1. accuse	_____	_____
2. exonerate	_____	_____
3. library	_____	_____
4. expedite	_____	_____
5. decide	_____	_____
6. depreciate	_____	_____
7. Canada	_____	_____
8. college	_____	_____
9. interrupt	_____	_____
10. episcopal	_____	_____

1. accusation	5. decision	9. interruption
2. exoneration	6. depreciation	10. Episcopalian
3. librarian	7. Canadian	
4. expedition	8. collegian	

17

Following are two lists of words. Study them. Pronounce them.

allowedly	basically
adequately	aesthetically
civilly	enthusiastically
faintly	hypothetically
expressly	scientifically
finely	microscopically
erectly	physically
abnormally	skeptically
loosely	pragmatically
perfectly	hectically

Can you draw a conclusion and discover your own principle for using *ly/ally?* Try here. ****_____
_____.

Anything that says:

Use *ally* **when the word or word root to which the suffix is being added ends in** *c;* **otherwise, use** *ly.*

Did you pronounce these words to see that *ly* and *ally* really sound alike?

18

There is one exception to the principle that you discovered—the word *public.* Democracy needs public_____ (*ly/ally*) minded people.

ly

19

A congressman might say, "I support this bill and want it on the record public_____."

ly

20

Privately means the opposite of *public_____.*

ly

21

Secretly also means the opposite of _____.

publicly

22

Secretly and *privately* mean the same thing. A word that means the opposite is _____.

publicly

23

The main principle (discovered in Frame 17) is, "**_____.**"

Use *ly* unless the word or word root ends in *c;* then use *ally.*

24

When the *changing-y-to-i* rule applies, use it. (This sequence is a review of Chapter 4.)

angry + ly becomes angrily
bloody + ly becomes _____

bloodily

25

crafty + ly becomes craftily
crazy + ly becomes _____
clumsy + ly becomes _____
dirty + ly becomes _____

crazily
clumsily
dirtily

26

fussy + ly becomes _____
jaunty + ly becomes _____
faulty + ly becomes _____
    but
coy + ly becomes _____

fussily
jauntily
faultily

coyly

27

The rule of final *e* (Chapter 2) still exists. Use it.

loose + ly becomes _____
love + ly becomes _____

loosely
lovely

28

Able becomes *ably.* Some words lose a syllable (drop the *e*) in becoming an adverb. *Listen to:*

comparable + ly = comparably
ample   + ly = amply
assemble + ly = assembly
irritable   + ly = irritably

Did it sound *am' ply* or *am' pel ly?*
as sem' bly or *as sem' bel ly?*
and so on.

29

You will spell words that drop an *e* before *ly* correctly if you **_____ words
correctly.

hear, listen to

30

The principle you discovered that governs the use
of *ly/ally* to form an adverb is, "**_____
_____."

After *c*, add *ally;*
otherwise, add *ly.*

31

Self-test

Form adverbs (*ly/ally*) from the words in Column I. Write the word in Column II.
Next, check your answers at the top of the next page. Correct any mistakes in
Column II. Write the correct word in Column III.

Column I	Column II	Column III
1. concrete		
2. clean		
3. faint		
4. civic		
5. scientific		
6. exact		
7. capable		
8. music		
9. musical		
10. abnormal		
11. accidental		
12. main		
13. logic		
14. logical		
15. partial		
16. private		
17. public		
18. secret		
19. specific		
20. gentle		

32

Did you ever see a word spelled
        chi*lly*, du*lly*, or fu*lly*?
Draw a conclusion. **_____
_____.

When a word ends in
ll, drop one *l* and add
ly.

DON'T MISS EVEN ONE OPPORTUNITY TO USE WHAT YOU HAVE LEARNED!

1. concretely
2. cleanly
3. faintly
4. civically
5. scientifically
6. exactly
7. capably (*Listen!*)
8. musically
9. musically
10. abnormally
11. accidentally
12. mainly
13. logically
14. logically
15. partially
16. privately
17. publicly
18. secretly
19. specifically
20. gently (*Listen!*)

8   suffixes: ify/efy— sede/ceed/cede

1

Pronounce the words *clas***sify** and *ra***refy**. Listen to the sound. When pronounced, the suffixes *ify/efy* sound **_____ (how).

alike, the same

2

Listen to *ify/efy* as you pronounce the words *qualify* and *stupefy*. When pronounced, *ify/efy* sound **_____ (how).

alike, the same
Did you hear it this time?

3

All but four verbs (to be presented later) that end in the *ify/efy* sound are spelled *ify*. To form a verb from *just*, use *ify/efy* and spell it _____.

justify

4

Using *ify/efy*, form verbs from the following:

humid _____	humidify
fort _____	fortify
class _____	classify
solid _____	solidify

5

Remember the rule of final *e* (Chapter 2) as you form verbs using *ify/efy* from the following:

ample _____	amplify
code _____	codify
type _____	typify
vile _____	vilify

6

Using *ify/efy*, form verbs from the following:

pure	_____
person	_____
acid	_____
note	_____

purify
personify
acidify
notify

7

To spell *ify/efy* words correctly, you need only learn four words and remember that all other words with this sound are spelled using _____.

ify

8

Some students learn better by memorization, others by using a memory aid. Use the method or device that best suits you to learn these four *efy* words.

A. Memorize:

   liquefy
   putrefy
   rarefy
   stupefy

B. Memory aid I:

The *putr*id *liqu*id *rare*ly *stupe*fies the smeller.

C. Memory aid II:

Look for the exception.
  i
    q
      u
        e
          f
        y

Read the exception.
  a
    r
      e
        f
          y

Study the exception.
  t
    u
      p
        e
          f
            y

Practice the exception.
  u
    t
      r
        e
          f
            y

9
Self-test

By adding *ify/efy*, build verbs from the word parts in Column I. In Column II, write the correct word. Next, check your answers at the bottom of the page. Correct any mistakes in Column II. Write your correct answers in Column III. Pronounce the word you are building.

Column I	Column II	Column III
1. beaut	_____	_____
2. cert	_____	_____
3. qual	_____	_____
4. sanct	_____	_____
5. divers	_____	_____
6. rar	_____	_____
7. ed	_____	_____
8. fals	_____	_____
9. stup	_____	_____
10. horr	_____	_____
11. putr	_____	_____
12. intens	_____	_____
13. typ	_____	_____
14. liqu	_____	_____
15. ver	_____	_____

1. beautify	6. rarefy	11. putrefy
2. certify	7. edify	12. intensify
3. qualify	8. falsify	13. typify
4. sanctify	9. stupefy	14. liquefy
5. diversify	10. horrify	15. verify

10

This is such a simple principle that you get a bonus for fun. This is a word-building, not a spelling, extra. (Word building always helps with spelling!)

11

The *tion* nouns are formed from *ify* verbs by changing the final *y* to *i* and adding *cation*. A noun built from *gratify* is _____.

gratification

12

Listen to sounds and syllables. A noun built from

    vilify   is vilification.
    identify is _____.

identification

    magnify is _____.

magnification

    unify   is _____.

unification

13

A noun built from

    versify is versification.
    ramify is _____.

ramification

    calcify is _____.

calcification

    glorify is _____.

glorification

14

A noun built from

    ratify   is _____.

ratification

    saponify is _____.

saponification

    simplify is _____.

simplification

    clarify is _____.

clarification

    modify is _____.

modification

15

Nouns built from *efy* words are formed by dropping the *y* and adding *action*. A noun built from *liquefy* is _____.

liquefaction
Listen to sounds!

16

Build nouns from the following *efy* verbs:

liquefy _____
rarefy _____
stupefy _____
putrefy _____

liquefaction
rarefaction
stupefaction
putrefaction

17

Build nouns from the following:

rectify _____
disqualify _____
emulsify _____
putrefy _____

rectification
disqualification
emulsification
putrefaction

Pronounce and listen!

18

Build nouns from the following:

exemplify _____
stupefy _____
liquefy _____
nullify _____

exemplification
stupefaction
liquefaction
nullification

19

When forming *tion* nouns from verbs ending in *efy*,
**_____.

Drop the *y* and add *action.*

20

When forming *tion* nouns from verbs ending in *ify*,
**_____.

Change the *y* to *i* and add *cation.*

21

All but four *ify/efy* verbs are spelled with _____.

ify

22

The four verbs that end in *efy* are _____,
_____, _____, and _____.

liquefy, stupefy, putrefy, rarefy

23

There are four word endings that have the sound of *seed*. A seed is something from which a plant will grow. Common sense tells you to spell *hayseed* with the _____ ending.

seed

24

Pumpkins will grow from a pumpkinseed. Cotton will grow from a _____.

cottonseed

25

By thinking of the meaning of the word, you can skip the ending *seed* and concentrate on learning the three endings *cede/ceed/sede.*

26

There is only one word that ends in *sede—supersede. Supersede* means to replace something or someone. The foreman's direction may be superseded by the manager's. The manager's order may be _____d by the department head's. The department head's direction may be _____d by the vice president's. The vice president's direction may be _____d by the president's. Even the president's memo may be _____ _____d by the chairman of the board. The chairman of the board is not likely to be _____ _____d until retirement. He, and the word _____, stand alone. There is only one *sede* word; it is _____.

supersede

supersede

supersede

supersede

supersede
supersede
supersede

27

There are three words that end in *ceed. Exceed, proceed,* and *succeed* all end with _____.

ceed

28

The eye may exceed the appetite.

The driver may _____ the speed limit. exceed

Your grades may _____ those of your exceed
sister or brother.

John's salary _____s Jim's. exceed

Jane's taste in clothes _____s her exceed
pocketbook.

Your own grades in one subject may _____ exceed
those in another.

29

Bob succeed(s) George as president of the class.

Mary _____s Jane as class secretary. succeed

Mr. Johns _____s Mr. White in succeed
office.

30

You can also succeed in something you have
undertaken.

My father is _____ing in business. succeed

My mother _____s in spending succeed
father's money.

I am determined to _____ at college. succeed

31

I will proceed to give you the directions. All cars
will drive to Brinkers Crossroads and then stop for
gas. From there, we will pro_____ to Norris- ceed
town and stop where the lead car stops. Then we
will pro_____ to Beltsville and lunch. After ceed
lunch, we will _____ to Mount proceed
Royale and stop for gas. We will then _____ proceed
to the Colonial Motor Inn on Route 711 where we
will rally for dinner and the night. The following
morning, I will _____ with the day's proceed
directions.

32

If you pro_____ to ex_____ the speed limit, you will probably suc_____ in getting a fine.

ceed, ceed
ceed

33

All "seed" words except those in frames 26 through 31 end in *cede*. Even the word *cede* follows the rule.

I con_____ you the victory.

cede

He will inter_____ on my behalf.

cede

The bride will pre_____ the bridesmaids to the altar.

cede

I will pre_____ my speech with some light remarks.

cede

Although Harry is only thirty years old, his hairline has already begun to re_____.

cede

34
Self-test

By adding cede/ceed/sede, build words from the word parts in Column I. In Column II, write the correct word. Next, check your answers at the bottom of the page. Correct any mistakes in Column II. Write your correct answers in Column III.

Column I	Column II	Column III
1. ac	_____	_____
2. con	_____	_____
3. super	_____	_____
4. pro	_____	_____
5. inter	_____	_____
6. pre	_____	_____
7. suc	_____	_____
8. re	_____	_____
9. se	_____	_____
10. ex	_____	_____
11. ante	_____	_____

1. accede	5. intercede	9. secede
2. concede	6. precede	10. exceed
3. supersede	7. succeed	11. antecede
4. proceed	8. recede	

9   prefixes

1

So far, you have been improving your spelling by learning some things about word roots and suffixes. A suffix is added to a word root to change
** _____ .

its meaning

2

Now for some information about prefixes. A *prefix* is placed before a * _____ to change its meaning.

word root (word)

3

In the words *im/plant, trans/plant,* and *sup/plant, im, trans,* and *sup* are _____ .

prefixes

4

In the words *im/port, trans/port,* and *sup/port, im, trans,* and *sup* are _____ .

prefixes

5

In frames 3 and 4, *plant* and *port* are * _____ .

word roots

6

A prefix is placed ** _____ in order to ** _____ .

before a word root
change its meaning

7

There are many prefixes in the English language. Unlike suffixes, prefixes change form. Examine the next page.

Just *read* this page and do what it tells you to do.

The prefix *sub* means "under" or "below."

> *Examples:*
>> sub/marine
>> sub/division

Before the letter *c, sub* becomes *suc.*

> *Examples:*
>> suc/ceed
>> suc/cess

Before *f, sub* becomes *suf.*

> *Examples:*
>> suf/fer
>> suf/fix

Before *g, sub* becomes *sug.*

> *Example:*
>> sug/gest

Before *m, sub* becomes *sum.*

> *Example:*
>> sum/mon

Before *p, sub* becomes *sup.*

> *Example:*
>> sup/port

Before *r, sub* becomes *sur.*

> *Example:*
>> sur/reptitious

Draw a conclusion:

Learning to spell *sub* words could be very complicated if you did not pronounce the words and **_____ the differences in the sounds of *sub* forms.

hear *or* listen to .

Many prefixes change form as *sub* did. These changes grew with our language. They added ease to pronunciation. Just read this page, then draw your conclusion.

The prefix *con,* which means "with," becomes *col, com, cor,* and *co.*
> (con/sent, con/nect, col/lege, com/ment, cor/rect, co/operate)

The prefix *di,* which means "apart" or "separation," becomes *dif, dis,* and *des.*
> (di/gest, dif/fer, dis/sect, des/sert)

The prefix *ex* ("out from" or "out of") becomes *ec* and *ef.*
> (ex/tract, ec/centric, ef/fect)

The prefix *in* ("into" or "not") becomes *il, im, ir, en,* and *em.*
> (in/sert, in/nocent, il/legal, im/mature, ir/regular, en/noble, em/pathy)

The prefix *ob* ("against" or "in the way") becomes *oc, of,* and *op.*
> (ob/ject, ob/bligato, oc/cur, of/fend, op/pose)

The prefix *syn* ("with") becomes *syl, sym,* and *sys.*
> (syn/onym, syl/lable, sym/metry, sys/tem)

Draw a conclusion:

Learning to spell prefixes could be very complicated if **_____.

I could not hear the sound.

If you are asking, "Why bother with prefixes since I can hear the sound?", go to frame 8 and start to learn an excellent reason.

8

Prefixes change form. A word root *does not*. Because a word root does not change form, you know when you hear the word *misspell* to spell it *mis/spell*—two *s*'s. *Mis/spell* means "to spell wrongly." The word for "taking a wrong step" is _____.

misstep

9

Since you know that word roots do not change form, you know to double the letter when the prefix ends in the same letter that starts the word root. A word for "speak wrongly" is _____.

misspeak

10

A word for "spend wrongly (improperly)" is _____. A word for "state wrongly (improperly)" is _____.

misspend
misstate

11

From the prefix *mis* and words beginning with *s*, you have learned that knowing about these changing forms of prefixes will help you spell correctly by _____ing the letter.

doubling

12

On a separate piece of paper, start a list of prefixes with their meanings and an example of each used in a word. Put on this list ONLY prefixes that give you a double letter when you use them.

13

The prefix *ad* means "to" or "toward." *Ad/duct* means "move _____." Build words from *ad*, plus

toward (to)

    dict _____

addict

    dress _____

address

    duce _____

adduce

14

The prefix *ad* _____ (should/should not) be added to your list.

should

15

Co, col, com, and *cor* mean "together" or "with." *Com/motion* means, literally, "with motion." *com + mand* is spelled _____.

command

Say it and listen.

16

Com means "*_____."

with *or* together

17

Build words from *com,* plus

memorate _____	commemorate
mence _____	commence
ment _____	comment
mit _____	commit

18

Build words from *con,* plus

nect _____	connect
(*literal meaning:* "fasten together")	
note _____	connote
nive _____	connive
nate _____	connate
(*literal meaning:* "born with")	

Con means "*_____."

with *or* together

19

Build words from *col,* plus

late _____	collate
league _____	colleague
lege _____	college
lide _____	collide
(*literal meaning:* "strike together")	

Col means "*_____."

together *or* with

20

Build words from *cor,* plus

rect	_____	correct
respond	_____	correspond
	(*literal meaning:* "answer together")	
rosion	_____	corrosion
rupt	_____	corrupt

Cor means "*_____." together *or* with

21

Build words from *co,* plus

op	_____	coop
	(*literal meaning:* "work together")	
operate	_____	cooperate
ordinate	_____	coordinate
ordination	_____	coordination

Co means "*_____." together *or* with

22

Build words from:

ad	+	dicted	_____	addicted
col	+	lapse	_____	collapse
com	+	mend	_____	commend
con	+	notation	_____	connotation
cor	+	relate	_____	correlate

23

Build words from:

co	+	optive	_____	cooptive
cor	+	rode	_____	corrode
col	+	lect	_____	collect
com	+	merce	_____	commerce
con	+	notation	_____	connotation

24

Are *co, col, com, con,* and *cor* on your list? These
are five forms of one prefix that means "*_____
_____." with *or* together

25

Di, dif, and *dis* mean "apart" or "separate." The literal meaning of *dis/satisfy* is "to separate from satisfaction." *Dis* + *seat* is spelled _____.

disseat

26

Build a word from *dis,* plus

sect	_____	dissect
	(*literal meaning:* "cut apart")	
sent	_____	dissent
similar	_____	dissimilar
solve	_____	dissolve

Dis means "*_____."

apart *or* separate

27

Build a word from *dif,* plus

fer	_____	differ
fuse	_____	diffuse
ficult	_____	difficult
fract	_____	diffract
	(*literal meaning:* "break apart")	

Dif means "*_____."

apart *or* separate

28

Build a word from *di,* plus

gest	_____	digest
lapidate	_____	dilapidate
	(*literal meaning:* "stone apart")	
mension	_____	dimension
rect	_____	direct

Di means "*_____."

apart *or* separate

29

Build words from:

dis + simulate	_____	dissimulate
dif + fraction	_____	diffraction
di + gress	_____	digress
dif + fidence	_____	diffidence
dis + sipate	_____	dissipate

30

Do you have *what you need* of *di, dif,* and *dis* on your list? *Di, dif,* and *dis* mean "*_____ _____.*"

apart *or* separate

31

In, il, im, and *ir* mean "in," "into," or "not." *In/numerable* means "not able to be numbered." *In + nate* is spelled _____.

innate

32

Build a word from *in,* plus

nocent	_____	innocent
	(*literally:* "not do wrong")	
novate	_____	innovate
	("alter in")	
nervate	_____	innervate
nominate	_____	innominate

In means "*_____.*"

in *or* not

33

Build a word from *im,* plus

mature	_____	immature
	("not mature")	
migrate	_____	immigrate
	("remove in")	
mediate	_____	immediate
material	_____	immaterial

Im means "*_____.*"

in *or* not

34

Build a word from *il,* plus

legal	_____	illegal
legible	_____	illegible
limitable	_____	illimitable
literate	_____	illiterate

Il means "*_____.*"

in *or* not

35

Build a word from *ir,* plus

rational	_____	irrational
	("not rational")	
regular	_____	irregular
remediable	_____	irremediable
reparable	_____	irreparable

Ir means "*_____."   in *or* not

36

Build a word from:

in	+	active	_____	inactive
in	+	noxious	_____	innoxious
il	+	logical	_____	illogical
im	+	mobile	_____	immobile
ir	+	rigate	_____	irrigate

37

Build a word from:

im	+	press	_____	impress
im	+	merse	_____	immerse
ir	+	reverence	_____	irreverence
in	+	numerous	_____	innumerous
in	+	appreciable	_____	inappreciable
il	+	lusion	_____	illusion

38

Do you have what you need of *in, im, il,* and *ir* on your list? *In, im, il,* and *ir* mean "*_____."   in, into, not

39

Inter means "between" or "among." *Inter/vene* means "to come between." *Inter/rupt* means, literally, "to break between." *Inter + play* is spelled _____. *Inter + related* is spelled _____.

interplay
interrelated

40

Build a word from *inter*, plus

fere	interfere
rogate	interrogate
("ask between")	
radial	interradial
cross	intercross

Inter means "*_____." | between *or* among

41

Build a word from *inter*, plus

relating	interrelating
rupted	interrupted
("break between")	
lace	interlace
state	interstate
breed	interbreed

Inter means "*_____." | between *or* among

42

Do you have *inter* on your list? *Inter* means
"*_____." | between *or* among

43

Ob, oc, of, and *op* mean "against" or "in the way."
Ob + *ject* means, literally, "to throw against."
Ob + *literate* is spelled _____. | obliterate

44

Build a word from *ob*, plus

struct	obstruct
("pile up against")	
stinate	obstinate
tain	obtain
serve	observe

Ob means "*_____." | against, in the way

45

Build a word from *ob,* plus

long	_____	oblong
fuscate	_____	obfuscate
	("darken against")	
bligato	_____	obbligato
lique	_____	oblique
Ob means "*	_____."	against, in the way

46

Build a word from *oc,* plus

casion	_____	occasion
cult	_____	occult
cupant	_____	occupant
cur	_____	occur
	("run against")	
Oc means "*	_____."	against, in the way

47

Build a word from *oc,* plus

clude	_____	occlude
	("shut against")	
cupy	_____	occupy
clusion	_____	occlusion
curring	_____	occurring
Oc means "*	_____."	against, in the way

48

Build a word from *of,* plus

fend	_____	offend
	("strike against")	
fence	_____	offence
fer	_____	offer
Of means "*	_____."	against, in the way

49

Build a word from *of,* plus

fensive	offensive
fered	offered
fending	offending
fenseless	offenseless

Of means "*_____."   against, in the way

50

Build a word from *op,* plus

ponent	opponent
portune	opportune
pose	oppose
posite	opposite

        ("position against")

Op means "*_____."   against, in the way

51

Build a word from *op,* plus

position	opposition
press	oppress
portunity	opportunity
pugn	oppugn

Op means "*_____."   against, in the way

52

Do you have what you need of *ob, oc, of,* and *op* on your list? *Ob, oc, of,* and *op* mean "*_____

_____."   against, in the way

53

Re means "again" or "back." *Re/echo* means "to echo again." *Re + enforce* is spelled _____.   reenforce

54

Build a word from *re,* plus

enter _____	reenter
("enter again")	
educate _____	reeducate
enact · _____	reenact
examine _____	reexamine

Re means "*_____." | again *or* back

55

Build a word from *re,* plus

employ _____	reemploy
fresh _____	refresh
edify _____	reedify
ject _____	reject
("throw back")	

Re means "*_____." | back *or* again

56

Does *re* belong on your list? _____ (yes/no) | *Yes, put it there.*

Re means "*_____." | back, again

57

Sub, suc, suf, sug, sum, sup, and *sur* mean "under" or "below." A *sub/basement* is a room under a basement. *Sub + bass* is spelled _____. | subbass

58

Build a word from *sub,* plus

plot _____	subplot
ject _____	subject
branch _____	subbranch
divide _____	subdivide
("divide under")	

Sub means "*_____." | under *or* below

59

Build a word from *suc,* plus

ceed _____	succeed
cinct _____	succinct
("grind under")	
cumb _____	succumb
cess _____	success

Suc means "*_____." | under *or* below

60

Build a word from *suf,* plus

fice _____	suffice
focate _____	suffocate
("below the throat")	
fuse _____	suffuse
ficient _____	sufficient

Suf means "*_____." | below *or* under

61

Build a word from *sug,* plus

gest _____	suggest
("carry under")	
gestion _____	suggestion
gestible _____	suggestible
gestibility _____	suggestibility

Sug means "*_____." | under *or* below

62

Build a word from *sum,* plus

mon _____	summon
("warn under")	
moner _____	summoner
moned _____	summoned
moning _____	summoning

Sum means "*_____." | under *or* below

63

Build a word from *sup,* plus

plement	supplement
port	support
("carry below")	
pose	suppose
pressive	suppressive

Sup means "*_____."   below *or* under

64

Build a word from *sur,* plus

reptitious	surreptitious
("seize under")	
reptitiously	surreptitiously
rogate	surrogate

Sur means "*_____."   under *or* below

65

Build a word from:

sup	+ plicate	supplicate
suf	+ ficient	sufficient
suc	+ cession	succession
sub	+ jugation	subjugation
sub	+ branching	subbranching

66

Do you have what you need of *sub, suc, sug, sum, sup,* and *sur* on your list? They all mean "*_____."

under *or* below

67

Trans means "across" or "over." *Trans + science* is spelled *transcience. Trans + sient* is spelled _____.

transient

68

Trans + sude is spelled *transude. Trans + spire* is spelled _____.

transpire

69

Build a word from *trans,* plus

scend	_____	transcend
scribe	_____	transcribe
	("write over or across")	
sect	_____	transect

Trans means "*_____." | over *or* across

70

Does *trans* belong on your list? _____ (yes/ no). *Trans* means "*_____."

no
across *or* over

71

Syn, sym, and *syl* mean "with" or "together." *Syn/ chronism* means, literally, "together in time." *Syn + onym* is spelled _____."

synonym

72

Build a word from *syn,* plus

copation	_____	syncopation
dicate	_____	syndicate
apse	_____	synapse
thesis	_____	synthesis

Syn means "*_____." | with *or* together

73

Build a word from *sym,* plus

pathy	_____	sympathy
	("with feeling")	
ptom	_____	symptom
metallic	_____	symmetallic
metrical	_____	symmetrical

Sym means "*_____." | with *or* together

74

Build a word from *sym,* plus

posium	_____	symposium
metallism	_____	symmetallism
phonic	_____	symphonic
phony	_____	symphony
	("sound together")	

Sym means "*_____." together *or* with

75

Build a word from *syl,* plus

lable	_____	syllable
	("hold or take together")	
labify	_____	syllabify
labus	_____	syllabus
logism	_____	syllogism

Syl means "*_____." together *or* with

76

Build a word from:

sym	+	metry	_____ symmetry
syl	+	labic	_____ syllabic
syn	+	copation	_____ syncopation
syn	+	tax	_____ syntax

77

Put what you need of *syn, sym,* and *syl* on your list.
Syn, sym, and *syl* mean "*_____." together, with

78

In your dictionary, find the prefix *ex.* It means
"*_____." from, out of

79

Read the following and think as you read:

Ex, e, ec, and *ef,* mean "from" or "out of."

ex	e
ex/amine	e/dict
ex/hibit	e/gress
ex/port	e/levate
ex/tort	e/merge
ex/cept	e/nunciate
ex/clude	e/rase
ex/crete	e/vict

ec	ef (before f)
ec/centric	ef/fluence
ec/clesiastic	ef/fort
ec/stasy	ef/fuse
ec/static	ef/ficient

80

Pronounce the words *except* and *eccentric.* Do the *exc* and *ecc* sound alike? _____ (yes/no)

yes

81

In your dictionary, notice how many of the words begin with *ex/c.* Now see how many words begin with *ec/c.* List the doubling *c* words you need to know from the dictionary. **_____ _____.

Eccentric, ecclesiastic and their forms are probably the only ones you need to know.

82

Using your dictionary, list five *ef/f* words in which *ef* means *ex.* **_____ _____ _____.

There are so many that I'm sure you are right.

83

Ex, e, ec, and *ef* mean "*_____.*"

from *or* out of

84

Which forms of *ex* (*e, ex, ec, ef*) belong on your list? **_____.

ec, ef

85

To be sure you have the prefixes you need on your list, check with the next page.

For Checking Your List of Prefixes

Prefix	Meaning	Example in Use
		(Give your own example.)

Prefix	Meaning
1. *mis*	"wrong"
2. *ad*	"to," "toward"
3. *co*	
4. *col*	
5. *com*	"together," "with"
6. *con*	
7. *cor*	
8. *dis*	"apart," "separate"
9. *dif*	
10. *in*	
11. *il*	"in," "into," "not"
12. *im*	
13. *ir*	
14. *inter*	"between," "among"
15. *ob*	
16. *oc*	"against," "opposed to"
17. *of*	
18. *op*	
19. *re*	"again," "back"
20. *sub*	
21. *suc*	
22. *suf*	
23. *sug*	"under," "below"
24. *sum*	
25. *sup*	
26. *sur*	
27. *sym*	"with," "together"
28. *syl*	
29. *ec*	"from"
30. *ef*	

Build a word using the following prefixes. Some will result in a double letter; some will not. Do all you can without a dictionary; then go back and finish the list using a dictionary.

ab ("from")

ad ("to," "toward")

circum ("around")

col ("together")

com ("together")

con ("together")

cor ("together")

co ("together")

dis ("apart," "separation")

dif ("apart," "separation")

di ("apart," "separation")

ex ("from," "out of")

e ("from," "out of")

ec ("from," "out of")

ef ("from," "out of")

in ("in," "into," "not")

il ("in," "into," "not")

im ("in," "into," "not")

ir ("in," "into," "not")

inter ("between")

ob ("against")

oc ("against")

of ("against")

op ("against")

re ("back," "again")

sub ("under," "below")

suc ("under," "below")

suf ("under," "below")

sug ("under," "below")

sum ("under," "below")

sup ("under," "below")

sur ("under," "below")

trans ("across," "over")

syn ("with")

sym ("with")

syl ("with")

sys ("with")

Where you are not certain, check your answers with a dictionary.

87

Study the following word lists and then draw a conclusion.

syn	*sym*
synchronism	symbiosis
synchromesh	symbol
syndicate	symbology
syndrome	symbolist
synergism	symmetallism
syngenetic	symmetric
synopsis	symmetry
synod	symmetrical
synonym	sympathy
syntax	symphonic
synthesis	sympodium
	symptom

Syn becomes *sym* before the letters ——, ——, and ——.

b, m, p

88

Another bonus!
A prefix can be put before a prefix.

Study:

    re com mend
    ac com modate
    re col lect

Add to your list as you meet more of these.

89

Another bonus if you want it!
If the prefix doubling principle has been helpful for you, work out a list of words using *ad*. (*Ad* becomes *ac, af, ag, al, an, ap, ar, as,* and *at*.) Take your dictionary. You're on your own!

10   sound-alike prefixes

1

Many prefixes, although spelled differently, sound alike or very nearly alike when pronounced normally. Do *for* and *fore* sound alike? _____ (yes/no)

yes

2

Pronounce *intermittent* and *intramural*. When pronounced normally do *inter* and *intra* sound similar? _____ (yes/no)

Most people think they do.

3

The sound of *pre* in the word *prerogative,* as it is normally pronounced, is indistinguishable from *per*. Students often fail to find it in the dictionary because they are looking under *per*.

Don't worry! This chapter will help with this type of problem.

4

In your dictionary, find the word *prerogative*. Notice that the pronunciation is given as *pri-rog'-ə-tiv*. The first syllable does not have a long *e* sound.

Say *prerogative* several times and listen to what you say.

5

Following the pronunciation of *prerogative,* the origin of the word is given in brackets [   ]. Reading to the end of the brackets, you find *prerogative* came from the Latin word parts *prae,* which means "_____" and *rogare,* which means "*_____."

before
to ask

6

If someone possesses something, "before asking," it is his *prerogative*. When you know that *pre* (from the Latin *prae*) means "before" and that *per* means "through," you are more likely to spell *pre/per* words ** _____ (how).

correctly, right

7

In this chapter, you will learn to pick the right prefix *most* of the time by knowing its meaning. As you practice thinking in terms of these few prefix meanings, your spelling will continue to improve for a very long time.

8

For and *fore* are pronounced the same way. Pronounce *foreground* and *forgive*. Do *for/fore* sound alike? _____ (yes/no)

yes

9

A *fore/ground* is the part nearest the viewer, the front part. A dog's *fore/foot* is one of his two _____ feet. *Fore* means "before" or "in _____ of."

front
front

10

One's *fore/head* is really the _____ part of his head. To have *fore/knowledge* of an event is to know about it _____ it happens.

front

before

11

The forearm is the _____ part of the arm.

front

12

The expression "weather forecast" means telling the weather _____ it happens.

before

13

The forenoon comes _____ noon.

before

14

The forebrain is the _____ part of the brain.

front

15

When playing tennis, a backhand stroke is made with the back of the hand leading. When the front of the hand leads, we call it a _____ stroke.

forehand

16

To pass judgment before the jury brings in a verdict is to _____judge the defendant.

fore(judge)

17

There is an expression, "Hindsight is better than _____."

foresight

18

For means "separate" ("away," "apart," "off") or "intensely" (very much). To *for/get* is to lose (separate) facts from the mind. To *for/bid* is to command to stay _____ from.

away *or* separate

19

To *for/swear* candy for Lent is to give up (be separated from) candy. To *for/go* something is to
**_____.

give it up *or* be separated from it

20

To *forfend* an event is to keep it from (separate it from) happening. *Forgive* means "to **_____ _____ resentment."

give up *or* separate from

21

The _____giver is the one who gives up resentment. The _____(en) is the one against whom resentment is given up.

for
forgiven

22

The person who loses (facts) from his mind is called _____getful. The facts that are lost or separated from the mind are _____gotten. The process of losing facts from the mind is _____(ing).

for
for

forgetting

23

One meaning of *for* is "**_____."

separate, away

24

Another less common meaning of *for* is "intensely." To *for/weep* is to weep intensely. To be *forlorn* is to be _____ lost.

intensely

25

To be *forspent* is to be intensely weary or exhausted. To be *forwearied* also means "to be *_____."

intensely weary *or* exhausted

26

Forever means, literally, "intensely ever." To *forwaste* means, literally, "to waste _____."

intensely

27

To *forsake* is to abandon, give up (separate from) something. That which is given up is _____ _____(en).

forsaken

28

In your dictionary, find the following words and write their meanings:

Word	Meaning	
1. forebear	**_____	ancestor, forefather
2. forbear	**_____	to refrain from
3. forebearer	**_____	ancestor, forefather
4. forbearer	**_____	one who refrains from

29

It is easy to see the connection between *fore* and *before* or *front*. The connections with *for* as *separate* or *intensely* are more difficult to see. If you ask, "Does this word mean 'before' or 'front'?" and it does, you will know how to spell it _____.

fore

30

If you ask yourself, "Does this word mean 'before' or 'front'?" and it doesn't, you will know to spell it _____.

for

31

If you make the association of *fore* with beFORE, you will know to use _____ (*for/fore*) if the meaning of the word implies *before*.

fore

32

One caution and one exception: The word *formal* is the adjective for *form*. The word *format* also comes from the word _____ rather than the prefix *for*.

form

33

Your caution is to remember there are many different words built from the word *form*. Not all words beginning with *for* are using the prefix

_____.

for

34

Do you really think you would have trouble seeing the *form* in the words *formal, formation, formative, formless* or *formula?* _____ (yes/no)

If you think so, use your dictionary and make a list of "form" words. Ask someone to check it with you.

35

Now for an exception: In your dictionary, find the word *forward* and read all of its meanings. All meanings of *forward* give a sense of **_____.

before *or* front

36

To avoid confusion of *forward* (the exception to your rule) and *foreword,* look up *foreword* in your dictionary. Its meaning follows the rule of _____ (*for/fore*).

fore

37

Another pair of sound-alike prefixes is *anti/ante.* An *anti/aircraft* gun shoots against (enemy) aircraft. An *anti/missile* missile is one that is propelled against an enemy missile. An *antiseptic* works against sepsis (infection). *Anti* means "_____."

against

38

An *antebellum* custom existed before the civil war. *Antediluvian* means "before the biblical flood." An *antecedent* refers to something that comes before. *Ante* means "_____."

before

39

Build a word meaning:

"something that detracts from (works against) the climax" _____

anticlimax

"something that prevents (works against) freezing" _____ (think of the noun)

antifreeze

"the room that comes before the main room"

_____

anteroom *or* antechamber

"a forward version (turning *or* placement)"

_____

anteversion

40

Antemortem means "_____ death."

before

Antipathy means "_____ feeling." (opposite of *sym/pathy*)

against

Antichrist means "*_____."

against Christ

Antecede means go "_____."

before

41

You can spell *anti/ante* words correctly by knowing their general meaning if you know that *anti*
means "_____" and *ante* means
"_____."

against
before

42

Look in your dictionary at the words beginning
with *anti,* then *ante.* There are many more words
beginning with _____ than with
_____.

anti
ante

43

Inter/intra is another pair of sound-alike prefixes.
To *inter/act* means "to act between (with) each
other." The word *interAmerican* means "between
the nations of North and South America." To
inter/lay means "to lay between." *Inter* means
"_____."

between

44

An *intramuscular* injection is a "shot" given within
a muscle. *Intra/state* means "within a state."
Something *intra/molecular* is acting or existing
within a molecule. *Intra* means "_____."

within

45

An injection given into (within) a vein is an
_____venous (*inter/intra*) injection. Space
between stars is _____stellar (*inter/intra*)
space.

intra
inter

46

Sports events occurring within a college are
_____mural sports. Something within a
nucleus is an _____nuclear substance.

intra
intra

47

An airplane trip between continents is an
_____al flight.

A treaty between nations is an _____
_____al treaty.

intercontinent

internation

48

You can spell *inter/intra* words correctly by knowing their general meaning if you know that *inter* means "_____" and *intra* means "_____."

between
within

49

Look in your dictionary at the words beginning with *inter*, then *intra*. There are many more words beginning with _____ than with _____.

inter
intra

50

Ab/ad can be a pair of sound-alike prefixes. When a child is *ab/ducted*, he is taken away from his parents. An *ab/errant* person is one who has wandered away from the typical. To *ab/hor* something is to shrink away from it in fear or disgust. *Ab* means "_____."

away from

51

An *ad/jective* is added to (a noun).
Ad/jacent means "close to (something)."
Ad/duction is movement to (toward the body).
Ad means _____.

to

52

To advise a person to (do something) is to _____monish (*ab/ad*) him. Writing attached to something is an _____script (*ab/ad*). To scrape the leather away from one's shoe is to _____rade (*ab/ad*) it.

ad
ad
ab

53

The first people to originate from an area are _____origines (*ab/ad*). A person who is away from what we think of as normal is called "_____."

ab

abnormal

54

You can spell *ab/ad* words correctly by knowing their general meaning if you know that *ab* means "_____" and *ad* means "_____."

from
to

55

Here is a gimmick to help you keep *ab/ad* straight:

When a child is kidnapped, he is taken away from his family—abducted.

Newspaper headlines do say, CHILD AB-DUCTED, don't they?

56

If *ab/duction* refers to taking *away from,* then *ad,* which is left, must mean "_____."

to

57

Per/pre are prefixes that can be confused. A *pre/fix* comes before the word root. To *pre/heat* the oven is to heat it before baking the pie. *Pre/historic* means "before (recorded) history." *Pre* means "_____."

before

58

Per/mit means, literally, "to let through." *Per/ambulate* means, literally, "to walk through." *Per/ceive* means, literally, "to take thoroughly." *Per/plex* means, literally, "to involve thoroughly." *Per* means "_____" and "_____."

through
thoroughly

59

A postage stamp that is cancelled before it is used is _____. A gift that is paid for before it is picked up is _____.

precancelled
prepaid

60

When you meet a friend through chance, you have met him _____. A book that is thoroughly durable is _____.

perchance
perdurable

61

To arrange a meeting for two friends before the event is to _____. A custom that was different before a war is a _____ custom.

prearrange
prewar

62

To cool a new refrigerator before putting food into it is to _____ the refrigerator. To judge the accused before his trial is to _____ him.

precool
prejudge

63
Self-test

Build a word using *pre/per* before the following word roots. *Say* and *listen* to the word you are building! Answers are at the bottom of the page.

pre means "before."
per means "through."
Per/chance the play,
I may pre/view.

Word Root	Literal Meaning	Word
1. forate	"bore through"	_____
2. pare	"get ready beforehand"	_____
3. dict	"tell before"	_____
4. tain	"hold thoroughly"	_____
5. mute	"change through"	_____
6. turb	"disturb through"	_____
7. natal	"before birth"	_____
8. position	"place before"	_____
9. view	"see before"	_____
10. severe	"persist through"	_____
11. suade	"urge through"	_____
12. cursor	"run before"	_____
13. cede	"move before"	_____
14. spective	"look through"	_____
15. lude	"play before"	_____

1. perforate	6. perturb	11. persuade
2. prepare	7. prenatal	12. precursor
3. predict	8. preposition	13. precede
4. pertain	9. preview	14. perspective
5. permute	10. persevere	15. prelude

64

Find examples in your dictionary, words that you have not already used, to complete the following chart. Pronounce the word carefully and hear what you say. Although it requires a lot of time to fill in this chart, doing it completely is the single MOST IMPORTANT part of this chapter.

Prefix	Literal Meaning	Prefix	Literal Meaning
for	"separate," "away"	*fore*	"before," "front"
		forequarter	front quarter
___	___	___	___
___	___	___	___
___	___	___	___
___	___	___	___
anti	*against*	*ante*	___
antifebrile	against fever		
___	___	___	___
___	___	___	___
___	___	___	___
___	___	___	___
inter	___	*intra*	___
___	___	___	___
___	___	___	___
___	___	___	___
___	___	___	___
ab	___	*ad*	___
___	___	___	___
___	___	___	___
___	___	___	___
___	___	___	___
per	___	*pre*	___
___	___	___	___
___	___	___	___
___	___	___	___
___	___	___	___

11   the intelligent guess

1

Usually when you try to write a word you can't spell, you look for it in the dictionary. Certainly if you are not sure of a word you are writing in a theme or business letter, you **_____.

Let's hope the answer was: "Look for it in a dictionary."

2

What happens when you are taking a test and cannot spell a word you want to use? **_____.

It could be fortunate that nobody sees that answer!

3

Let's face it. Even good spellers have to take an occasional guess. The difference between the good speller and the poor speller is that one guess is an intelligent _____.

guess

4

Of course, you should not guess if you can apply a **_____.

rule, system, principle, or use a dictionary

5

There are no rules or systems that apply to everything in spelling. In the English language, even one sound can be spelled in different ways. How many different vowels does the sound ə represent? _____

five: *a, e, i, o, u*

6

A good place to begin is with something familiar. This will not be a foolproof thing. It is one way to chance an intelligent _____. Everything in this chapter will give you more than a 50/50 chance, but will still be a _____.

guess

guess

7

Extend the principle of hard and soft *c* and *g*. *C* and *g* have a soft sound before the vowels ___ and ___. The sound of *c* and *g* is hard before the vowels ___ and ___.

e i
a o

8

Actually to say that the sound of *c* and *g* is USUALLY hard before *a, o, u,* and *consonants* is more nearly correct. Also, it is more accurate to say that the sound of *c* and *g* is USUALLY soft before ___, ___, and *y*.

e, i

9

The sound of the italicized *c* in the words

*c*yclone	is a	_____ (hard/soft) sound	soft
*c*ivic	is a	_____ (hard/soft) sound	soft
*c*lutter	is a	_____ (hard/soft) sound	hard
*c*ross	is a	_____ (hard/soft) sound	hard

10

The sound of *g* in the words

gypsy	is a	_____ (hard/soft) sound	soft
gymnasium	is a	_____ (hard/soft) sound	soft
greet	is a	_____ (hard/soft) sound	hard
glory	is a	_____ (hard/soft) sound	hard

11

Average to poor spellers frequently have difficulty with the words *angel/angle*. What happens when you want to spell one of these words and you apply the hard/soft sound principle? **_____
_____.

Any answer that makes a heavenly being *gel* and a corner *gle*.

12

There is no way to use the accent-shift principle with the word *longətude*. If you pronounce this word and *hear* the soft *g*, you will have about a 75/25 chance in your favor to spell it correctly. Spell it _____.

longitude

13

You can't shift the accent in the word *rigǝr* to find the correct vowel. If you pronounce *rigǝr,* and hear the hard *g,* you have a better-than-chance system to spell it correctly. Spell *rigǝr* _____.

rigor

14

Pronounce and listen to the following lists:

cat	gat
cot	got
cut	gut
crop	glob

C and *g* have a hard sound when followed by ___, ___, ___ or a _____.

a, o, u
consonant

15

Pronounce and listen to:

cession	genius
cistern	ginger
cyst	gypsy

C and *g* have a soft sound when followed by ___, ___, and ___.

e, i, y

16

Remember, this is a *guessing* device. It is an intelligent guess because it is USUALLY true. There are words like *gift, gilt,* and *girl.* In a few words, *g* (even if followed by *i*) has a _____ sound.

hard

17

Pronounce and listen to the following lists:

call	gam
cell	gem
cilia	gin
cold	gone
cuff	gull
cylinder	gym
cram	grim

Surely you can hear the sound by now.

18

To extend this concept, *look* at, *study, say* and *hear* the following:

rag	rang	tic
rage	range	ice

Even at the end of a word you need a softening vowel to have a soft sound for ___ or ___.

c, g

19

Study, say, and hear the following:

mica	sag	lac	mac
mice	sage	lace	mace
	saga	lactic	macron

20

Try:

age	cynic	hug
egg	cynical	huge
ace	cynicism	Hugo
act		

Do you think you can now apply this? _____ (yes/no)

21
Self-test

Pronounce the word in Column I. Listen to the sound of *c* or *g*. A vowel with the sound of ə follows the *c* or *g*. Supply the correct vowel after you have pronounced the word. Check your answers at the bottom of the page, then write the correct word in Column II.

Column I	Column II
1. ag___nt	_____
2. dang___r	_____
3. ag___le	_____
4. antic___pate	_____
5. ac___demic	_____
6. merg___r	_____
7. mang___r	_____
8. ag___ny	_____
9. dec___lorize	_____
10. advoc___cy	_____
11. ag___te	_____
12. ang___lar	_____
13. ag___tation	_____
14. ag___nize	_____
15. c___rric___lum	_____

1. agent	6. merger	11. agate
2. danger	7. manger	12. angular
3. agile	8. agony	13. agitation
4. anticipate	9. decolorize	14. agonize
5. academic	10. advocacy	15. curriculum

If you were right half the time, feel good. After all, what you have just done depends upon your vocabulary and will grow as your vocabulary grows.

22

Here is another approach to the intelligent guess.

able/ible

Study the following, then use it to work frames 23 through 35. This was prepared from a list of over 250 *able* words and 230 *ible* words.

1. To keep the sound of *c* or *g* hard, use *able*.

    Examples:
    applicable
    eradicable

    No exceptions on list.

1. To keep the sound of *c* or *g* soft, use *ible*. *Odds:* 3 to 1.

    Examples:
    eligible
    legible

    Number of words on list using *ible* for soft *c* or *g:* 35.

    Exceptions: the *ible/able* sound can be spelled *eable* to keep soft *c* or *g. Number of words on list:* 11.

    Examples:
    changeable
    serviceable

2. If you can add *ation* to the word root, use *able*.

    Examples:
    consider/able
            /ation
    imit/able
         /ation

    Number of applications on list: over 75.

    Exception: sens/ible
                  sens/ation

    75 to 1 is well beyond chance.

2. If you can add *ion, ition,* or *ive* to the word root, use *ible*.

    Examples:
    defens/ible
           /ive
    depress/ible
            /ion
    add/ible
        /ition

    Number of applications on list: over 130.

    7 exceptions.

    130 to 7 is well beyond chance.

23

Build a word from:

applic	+ ible/able	_____	applicable
amic	+ ible/able	_____	amicable
fatig	+ ible/able	_____	fatigable
revoc	+ ible/able	_____	revocable

24

Build a word from:

convinc	+ ible/able	_____	convincible
elig	+ ible/able	_____	eligible
forc	+ ible/able	_____	forcible
tang	+ ible/able	_____	tangible

25

Build a word from:

despic	+ ible/able	_____	despicable
reduc	+ ible/able	_____	reducible
navig	+ ible/able	_____	navigable
leg	+ ible/able	_____	legible

26

Build a word from:

induc	+ ible/able	_____	inducible
intellig	+ ible/able	_____	intelligible
eradic	+ ible/able	_____	eradicable
evinc	+ ible/able	_____	evincible

27

The word root of *admirəble* is *admir*. Can you add *ation* to *admir* to form a word? The word is

_____.

admiration

28

If you hear the word *admirəble* and think of *admiration*, you know to spell *admir* + *ible/able*

_____.

admirable

29

The word root of *collectəble* is *collect.* Can you add *ion* to *collect* to form a word? The word is

_____.

collection

30

If you hear the word *collectəble* and think of *collection,* you know to spell *collect* + *ible/able*

_____.

collectible

31

The word root of *partəble* is *part.* Can you add *ition* to *part* to form a word? The word is

_____.

partition

32

When you hear the word *partəble* and think of *partition,* you know to spell *part* + *ible/able*

_____.

partible

33

Build a word from:

imit	+ ible/able	_____
demonstr	+ ible/able	_____
divis	+ ible/able	_____
respons	+ ible/able	_____

imitable (ation)
demonstrable (ation)
divisible (ion-ive)
responsible (ive)

34

Build a word from:

dissect	+ ible/able	_____
aud	+ ible/able	_____
flex	+ ible/able	_____
restor	+ ible/able	_____

dissectible (ion)
audible (ition)
flexible (ion)
restorable (ation)

35

Build a word from:

habit	+ ible/able	_____
illeg	+ ible/able	_____
vis	+ ible/able	_____
deduc	+ ible/able	_____

habitable
illegible (soft *g*)
visible
deducible

36
Self-test: *ible/able*

Using the word root in Column I + *ible/able*, write the correct word in Column II. Next, check your answers at the end of the frame. Correct any mistakes in Column II. Write your correct answers in Column III.

	Column I	Column II	Column III
1.	ador	_____	_____
2.	convers	_____	_____
3.	divis	_____	_____
4.	defens	_____	_____
5.	dur	_____	_____
6.	consider	_____	_____
7.	illeg	_____	_____
8.	add	_____	_____
9.	educible	(pronounce soft *c*)	*meaning:* "able to be educed"
10.	educable	(pronounce hard *c*)	*meaning:* "able to be _____"

1. adorable (will take *ation*)
2. conversable
3. divisible (will take *ion* or *ive*)
4. defensible (will take *ive*)
5. durable
6. considerable
7. illegible (soft *g*)
8. addible (will take *ition*)
9. educe—a verb meaning "to bring out something latent"
10. educated

37
If you miss this frame, it doesn't matter. If you have it right, feel good! Read the following two sentences:

The *mucus* secreted by the nose was clear.

Her *mucous* membrane was infected.

What are two differences between the *italicized* words? **_____
_____.

Muc/*us* is a noun.
Muc/*ous* is an adjective.

38
Read the following:

The radi*us* is one-half diameter of a circle.
The nerv*ous* child is crying.

Radi*us* is a _____ (noun/adjective)
Nerv*ous* is a _____ (noun/adjective)

noun
adjective

39

Read the following:

> Our cens*us* is taken every ten years.

> The obvi*ous* answer may be correct.

When spelling the *us/ous* sound, use
_____ if spelling a noun,   us
_____ if spelling an adjective.   ous

40

In the following sentences insert *us/ous* where indicated.

1. The boys chor___ will rehearse tonight.   us
2. The camp___ is decorated for the festival. us
3. A moment___ decision was reached.   ous
4. The notori___ criminal was apprehended.   ous

41

In the following sentences insert *us/ous* where indicated.

1. In early spring croc___ blooms.   us
2. Jane is having trouble with her sin___.   us
3. Our office receives a yearly bon___.   us
4. The prickly pear is a common cact___.   us

42

In the following sentences insert *us/ous* where indicated.

1. Soil for violets should be rich in hum___.   us
2. She told a humor___ story.   ous
3. In the movie, terror was continu___.   ous
4. It was a rigor___ test.   ous
5. The clamor___ circ___ came to town.   ous, us

43

The following is *usually* true (min*us* can be a preposition, noun or adjective):

us is a _____ (noun/adjective) suffix.   noun
ous is a _____ (noun/adjective) suffix.   adjective

44

When spelling words with the *us/ous* sound, you will be correct most of the time if you end adjectives with _____ and nouns with _____.

    callus—*noun*
    callous—_____

ous
us
adjective

45

Extending the noun/adjective principle, it can be useful when guessing *al* from *el* or *le*. If you actually *need* to guess the suffix, you will be right about 80 per cent of the time by using *al* when spelling an adjective. Form an adjective from *critic*.

_____

critical

46

Build adjectives from the following by using an intelligent guess.

    1. His cultur____ background was good.
    2. The patient's ment____ reactions were sharp.
    3. John's opinion was considered radic____.
    4. The movie's production was coloss____.

al
al
al
al

47

Using the intelligent guess, build the following indicated words.

    1. A brut____ crime was committed.
    2. Addition____ information is needed.
    3. He is a casu____ acquaintance.
    4. The mor____ approach was adopted.
    5. The mor____ is clearly evident.

All end in *al* even though *moral* is a noun and an adjective.

48

You increase your 80/20 odds in guessing *al* when you realize that 90 per cent of *el/le* words are nouns or verbs. Using *al/el*, complete the following:

They were married in a small chap____.

> el

49

Complete the following sentences using the intelligent guess.

1. I marv____ at his wisdom.
2. They threw in the tow____.
3. The ex-prisoner rev____ed in his freedom.
4. The party was an annu____ event.

> el
> el
> el
> al

50

Complete the following:

1. It was an abnorm____ situation.
2. The situation was abnorm____.
3. "Ship of the desert" refers to the cam____.
4. You must chann____ the information through a centr____ office.

> al
> al
> el
> el
> al

51

Complete the following:

1. The mod____ wore a pinkish-blue dress.
2. He learned to mod____ in clay.
3. It was a mod____ airplane.
4. The *al/el* method is only a guess. This is evident because the word *model* can be a

_____, _____ or _____ (part of speech).

> el
> el
> el
>
> noun, verb, or adjective

52

BONUS: Also use your *c g* principle with

ance/ence
ant/ent.
ancy/ency.

53

Now to tackle the problem of *el/le!*

There are more *cel, cle, gel, gle* words than you would be likely to guess! For review, pronounce and listen to the following two lists:

angel	angle
chancel	miracle
cancel	bicycle
cudgel	bungle

el/le

To keep the sound of *c* or *g* soft, use_____.   el

To keep the sound of *c* or *g* hard, use _____.   le

C or *g* has a soft sound before ___, ___, and ___.   *e, i,* and *y*

C or *g* has a hard sound before ___, ___, ___, and   *a, o, u,*

_____.   and consonants

54

What about other *el/le* words? Following is an aid that can be a big help:

Use *el* after:

v *example:* level
    odds: nearly 100 percent

r *example:* laurel
    odds: nearly 100 percent

s *example:* morsel
    odds: 7 to 1

w *example:* towel
    odds: nearly 100 percent

Although the following give you nearly 100 percent chance of being correct, they have fewer applications.

n *example:* panel

m *example:* trammel

h *example:* satchel

Use *le* after:

vowels (*a, e, i, o, u*)
    example: missile, schedule
    odds: 9 to 1, including proper nouns
    30 to 1, excluding proper nouns

b (excluding *ible/able*)
    example: amble, marble
    odds: 8 to 1, including proper nouns
    15 to 1, excluding proper nouns

d *example:* poodle, meddle
    odds: 15 to 1

k *example:* ankle, pickle
    odds: 18 to 1

f *example:* ruffle, sniffle
    odds: nearly 100 percent

t *example:* bottle
    odds: 8 to 1

p *example:* sample
    odds: only 3 to 1

Although the following give you nearly 100 percent chance of being correct, they have fewer applications.

z *example:* puzzle

y *example:* style

MEMORY AIDS

reverse! win him!

All consonants in the above are USUALLY followed by *el*.

fake tip—be dizzy!

All consonants in the above are USUALLY followed by *le*.

55
Self-test

Complete the blanks in Column I. Check your answers at the bottom of the page; then write the entire, correct word in Column II.

Column I	Column II
1. mang___r	_____
2. vic___r	_____
3. abrog___te	_____
4. offic___r	_____
5. revoc___ble	_____
6. invinc___ble	_____
7. indefatig___ble	_____
8. neglig___ble	_____
9. abomin___ble	_____
10. admiss___ble	_____
11. part___ble	_____
12. alter___ble	_____
13. fus___ble	_____
14. cynic_____ (al/el/le)	_____
15. cutic_____ (al/el/le)	_____
16. canc_____ (al/el/le)	_____
17. nerv_____ (us/ous)	_____
18. extravag_____ (ance/ence)	_____
19. intellig_____ (ance/ence)	_____
20. signific_____ (ance/ence)	_____

1. man*ge*r—soft *g*
2. vi*ca*r—hard *c*
3. abro*ga*te—hard *g*
4. offi*ce*r—soft *c*
5. revo*ca*ble—hard *c*
6. invin*ci*ble—soft *c*
7. indefati*ga*ble—hard *g*
8. negli*gi*ble—soft *g*
9. abomin*a*ble—will take *ation*
10. admiss*i*ble—will take *ion*
11. part*i*ble—will take *ition*
12. alter*a*ble—will take *ation*
13. fus*i*ble—will take *ion*
14. cynic*al*—adjective and hard *c*
15. cuti*cle*—noun and hard *c*
16. can*cel*—verb and soft *c*
17. ner*vous*—adjective
18. extravag*ance*—hard *g*
19. intellig*ence*—soft *g*
20. signific*ance*—hard *c*

Finale for Fun (optional, of course)

56

It is a fairly safe bet, if you are (or were) a poor speller, that you have not played many word games. There are many such games that can be fun. For one to play by yourself or in competition with another, try this.

Game 1. Build as many words as you can from a word that causes you spelling difficulty.
Try—
TEMPERAMENT (You should look up the meaning if you don't know it.)

tea
tee
ten
term
tempt

After you have built all you can or care to, see the next page.

Here are many, but not all, of the words to be found in TEMPERAMENT. Surely, by now, you could not misspell *temperament!*

ten	tramp	parent	emmet
tent	tram	part	epee
tenet	trap	pat	eta
tea	treat	pane	rat
tear	tree	pate	rate
team	trepan	pant	ran
term	meant	patter	rant
tempt	meat	patent	ram
tempter	men	pan	rap
temper	man	pare	rape
tempera	map	preman	ramp
temperate	mar	prename	rare
tee	mare	amen	rapt
teem	mat	ament	ream
teen	mate	ampere	reap
teeter	matter	amp	reman
tepee	mean	ant	rent
tar	mane	ante	rep
tam	pram	ate	repeat
tan	prate	are	repeater
tap	permanent	arm	repent
tape	permeate	apt	ret
tame	per	ape	neat
tare	pert	art	net
tarp	pen	ear	nap
tat	pent	earn	nape
taper	pep	eat	near
tamer	par	ere	neap
tamp	nee	era	name

Game 2. When finding words in words you can make an extensive search as with *temperament,* or you can look for words of any length you decide upon. The point is to have fun and also learn to spell the difficult word. The final authority for the word's existence or spelling is your dictionary. It is wise to know the word's meaning and part of speech (noun/verb/adjective). Here are some more words that often cause spelling difficulty. Play with them or some word that causes you trouble.

chauffeur
columns
familiar
mysterious
peculiarities
resources
rhythm! (There is at least one word.*)
sophomore

57

Daily papers almost always have crossword puzzles. Try them for fun. Don't start with those in Sunday papers, for they are hardest. Wait a long while before you tackle the crossword puzzle in Sunday's *New York Times.*

Try some.

58

Scrabble and anagrams are two good word games to play with another person.

Keep them in mind.
Play them.

* (myth)

review   Chapter 1

Keep this page for review. Use it whenever
a rule is becoming difficult to remember or
apply.

In Column II, write the correct word. Next, check your answers at the bottom of
the page. Correct any mistakes in Column II. Write correct answers in Column III.

Column I	Column II	Column III
1. brag + art		
2. compel + ing		
3. account + ing		
4. adjourn + ment		
5. paper + ed		
6. patrol + er		
7. action + able		
8. defer + ed		
9. defer + ment		
10. transfer + able		

The rule you have been using to work this page is,
"Double the final consonant when **＿＿＿＿＿
＿＿＿＿＿＿＿＿＿＿＿＿＿＿＿＿＿＿＿＿＿＿.

the word is one sylla-
ble or the accent oc-
curs on the last sylla-
ble of the word or
word root."

controlling conditions:

1. **＿＿＿＿＿＿＿＿＿＿＿＿＿＿＿＿＿

1. The root ends in
single consonant pre-
ceded by single vowel.

2. **＿＿＿＿＿＿＿＿＿＿＿＿＿＿＿＿＿

2. The suffix begins
with a vowel.

1. braggart	6. patroller
2. compelling	7. actionable
3. accounting	8. deferred
4. adjournment	9. deferment
5. papered	10. transferable

review   Chapter 2

In Column II, write the correct word. Next, check your answers at the bottom of the page. Correct any mistakes in Column II. Write correct answers in Column III.

Column I	Column II	Column III
1. abbreviate + ion	_____	_____
2. active + ly	_____	_____
3. acquire + ing	_____	_____
4. toe + ing	_____	_____
5. adhere + ence	_____	_____
6. virtue + al	_____	_____
7. aware + ness	_____	_____
8. courage + ous	_____	_____
9. argue + ment	_____	_____
10. judge + ment	_____	_____

1. Drop final silent *e* when **_____
   _____.

2. Keep final silent *e* when **_____
   _____.

1. The suffix begins with a vowel.
2. The suffix begins with a consonant.

1.	abbreviation	6.	virtual
2.	actively	7.	awareness
3.	acquiring	8.	courageous
4.	toeing		(*exception*)
	(*exception*)	9.	argument
5.	adherence		(*exception*)
		10.	judgment
			(*exception*)

review   Chapter 3
(answers at bottom of page)

Rule 1: With the _____ sound of *e*, the rule is, "*i* before *e* except after ___."

Rule 2: Following sound of *sh* or *ch*, use _____ (*ie/ei*).

Rule 3: With the split sound of *ie/ei*, use _____.

Rule 4: All other sounds of *ie/ei* are spelled with _____.

Rule 1—exceptions:

There was a young sh_____k, an Iraqi,
Who was a wild, w_____rd, hep disc jockey.
With n_____ther sleep nor l_____sure
He suffered a s_____zure,
Which _____ther meant rest or be rocky.

A financ_____r is a good fr_____nd to have.

Rule 4—exceptions:

The girl with the s_____ve sifting sand by the sea
Is making a sand pie for a fr_____nd and for me.
Her fr_____nd, the l_____utenant, was heard to mutter, then cry,
"In l_____u of a pie, I shall lie down and die."
Now tie this together, explain it to me;
Must I eat a sand pie while watching the sea?

Rule 1:	Rule 3:	Rule 1—exceptions:
long	ie	all *ei* in the limerick
c		*ie* for the statement
Rule 2:	**Rule 4:**	**Rule 4—exceptions**
ie	ei	all *ie*

review   Chapter 3

(answers at bottom of page)

Rule 1: With the long sound of *e*, the rule is, "**_____

_____."

Rule 2: Following the sounds *ch* and *sh*, use _____.

Rule 3: With the split sounds of *ie/ei*, use **_____

_____.

Rule 4: All other sounds of *ei/ie*, **_____

Rule 1—exceptions:

_____   _____

_____   _____

_____   _____

_____

Rule 4—exceptions:

_____

_____

_____

_____

Rule 1:
 i before *e* except after *c*

Rule 2:
 ie

Rule 3:
 ie

Rule 4:
 use *ei*

Rule 1—exceptions:
 sheik, weird, neither,
 either, leisure, seize,
 financier

Rule 4—exceptions
 sieve
 friend
 lieutenant
 lieu

review   Chapter 3

(answers at bottom of page)

sheik
weird
leisure
1. neither   are exceptions to the rule **_____
seize   _____.
either
financier

2. *Chief* is an example of the rule **_____
_____.

3. *Quiet* and *science* are examples of the rule **_____
_____.

sieve
4. friend   are exceptions to the rule **_____
lieutenant _____.
lieu

---

1. *i* before *e* except after *c* when the sound of *e* is long
2. Following the sounds of *sh* or *ch*, use *ie*.
3. When the *ie/ei* sound is a split sound, spell the sound *ie*.
4. All other sounds of *e* that use the *ie/ei* combination are spelled *ei*.

review   Chapter 4

(answers at bottom of page)

In Column II, write the correct word. Next, check your answers at the bottom of the page. Correct any mistakes in Column II. Write correct answers in Column III.

Column I	Column II	Column III
1. accompany + ing	_____	_____
2. justify + able	_____	_____
3. comply + ance	_____	_____
4. beauty + ous	_____	_____
5. delay + ing	_____	_____
6. heavy + ly	_____	_____
7. deploy + ment	_____	_____
8. pity + ful	_____	_____
9. pity + ous	_____	_____
10. lonely + ness	_____	_____

The rules you have been using are:

1. Change final *y* to *i* when ** _____
   _____
   _____.

2. Keep the final *y* when ** _____
   _____.

3. Exceptions are ** _____.

1. accompanying
2. justifiable
3. compliance
4. beauteous
5. delaying
6. heavily
7. deployment
8. pitiful
9. piteous
10. loneliness

1. *a.* *y* is preceded by a consonant.
   b. before all endings except those beginning with *i*.
2. *y* is preceded by a vowel.
3. the *eous* words.

review   Chapter 5

(answers at bottom of page)

1. Most nouns are made plural by **_____

2. Common and proper nouns ending in the sound of *s* are pluralized by **_____.

3. Letters and numbers are pluralized by **_____.

4. Nouns ending in *y:*
   a. If *y* is preceded by a vowel, **_____.
   b. If *y* is preceded by a consonant, **_____.
   c. All proper nouns ending in *y* are made plural by **_____.

5. Nouns ending in *o* are *usually* made plural by **_____.

review   Chapter 6

Do you remember ə?

I hope you have been using the accent shift principle with ə regularly. If so, you should have an impressive list of key words at your command. As a review of Chapter 6, make a list on this page of your own key words and the words for which they are a key. If you are working this program in connection with a regular class, your teacher may even want to check this list to see how well you are progressing.

Key word:	*is the key to:*
1. spectacular	spectacle
2. notation	notary, notarize
3.	
4.	
5.	
6.	
7.	
8.	
9.	
10.	
11.	
12.	
13.	
14.	
15.	

review   Chapters 7 and 8

(answers at bottom of page)

1. The four words that end in *efy* are _____, _____, _____, and _____.

2. one *sede,* the word _____.
   three *ceed,* the words _____, _____, and _____.

   all other "seed" words spelled _____.

3. Words ending in *c* take _____ (*ly/ally*).
   Exception: the word _____.

4. _____ (*ion/ian*) means *one who.*
   _____ (*ion/ian*) indicates action or condition.

review   Chapters 9 and 10

In Column II, write the correct word. Next, check your answers at the bottom of the page. Correct any mistakes in Column II. Write correct answers in Column III.

Column I	Column II	Column III
1. con + note		
2. dis + solve		
3. il + legal		
4. inter + relate		
5. ob + serve		
6. suf + fuse		
7. im + material		
8. trans + scribe		
9. sup + port		
10. syl + lable		

Column I contains a list of words with the prefix italicized. Column II has a space for you to write the meaning of the italicized prefix. Check your answers at the bottom of the page. Correct any errors.

Column I

Column II (literal meaning)

1. *fore*cast   "carry _____"
2. *anti*pathy   "_____ feeling"
3. *per*cussion   "striking _____"
4. *inter*cede   "go _____"
5. *pre*rogative   "ask _____"
6. *ab*duct   "lead _____"
7. *pre*position   "place _____"
8. *ante*cede   "go _____"
9. *intra*muscular   "_____ muscle"
10. *ad*duce   "lead _____"

review   Chapter 11
intelligent guess

(answers at bottom of page)

1. After a hard *c* or *g,* the letter should be ___, ___, ___, or a _____.

2. After a soft *c* or *g,* the letter should be ___, ___, or ___.

3. For spelling nouns with a suffix that indicates *ability:* If you can add *ation* to the word root, use _____. If you can add *ion, ition,* or *ive* to the word root, use _____.

4. The following suffixes are usually used to spell what part of speech?

        us _____

        ous _____

        al _____

5. The consonants in the gimmick phrase "reverse! win him," are almost always followed by _____ *el/le.*

6. All vowels plus the consonants in the gimmick phrase "fake tip—be dizzy," are usually followed by _____ *el/le.*

1. *a o u*   consonant
2. *e i y*
3. able ible
4. noun   adjective   adjective
5. el
6. le

final self-test—covers all chapters

(answers at bottom of page)

		Spell in this column	Key word in this column
1.	admənit_____ (ion/ian)	_____	_____
2.	defənit_____ (ion/ian)	_____	_____
3.	məmmal_____ (ion/ian)	_____	_____
4.	finənc_____r (ie/ei)	_____	_____
5.	fənancial	_____	_____
6.	defənite + ly/ally	_____	_____
7.	politic_____ (ly/ally)	_____	
8.	_____sorted (a/as)	_____	
9.	_____scription (pre/per)	_____	
10.	con_____ (sede/ceed/cede)	_____	
11.	sign_____ (ify/efy)	_____	
12.	archang_____ (al/el/le)	_____	
13.	apologetic_____ (al/el/le)	_____	
14.	tang_____ (able/ible)	_____	
15.	applic_____ (able/ible)	_____	
16.	adolesc_____ (ance/ence)	_____	
17.	signific_____ (ant/ent)	_____	
18.	octop_____ (us/ous)	_____	
19.	hazard_____ (us/ous)	_____	
20.	suffic_____nt (ie/ei)	_____	
21.	compel + ing	_____	
22.	judge + ment	_____	
23.	active + ly	_____	
24.	duty + ous	_____	
25.	glory + ous	_____	
26.	church_____ (s/es)	_____	
27.	potato_____ (s/es)	_____	
28.	s_____ze (ie/ei)	_____	
29.	attorne_____ (ys/ies)	_____	
30.	alto_____ (s/es)	_____	

Spelling	Key word	Spelling	Spelling
1. admonition	admonish	11. signify	21. compelling
2. definition	define	12. archangel	22. judgment
3. mammalian	mammal	13. apologetical	23. actively
4. financier	financial	14. tangible	24. duteous
5. financial	financier	15. applicable	25. glorious
6. definitely	define	16. adolescence	26. churches
7. politically		17. significant	27. potatoes
8. assorted		18. octopus	28. seize
9. prescription		19. hazardous	29. attorneys
10. concede		20. sufficient	30. altos